PRA

# STRONG, BRAVE & BEAUTIFUL

"In the pages of Strong, Brave & Beautiful, you will find a chorus of voices singing this message over you: You are enough. The Kindred Mom writers share their stories with vulnerability, grace, and humor, and in doing so, they welcome you into a vision of motherhood that is at once honest and hopeful. Even on the hardest day, when you are up to your eyeballs in diapers and dishes, these ladies will be your village, reminding you that your efforts are not wasted. They will reorient you to the truth that you are, in fact, strong, brave, and beautiful."

—**Brittany L. Bergman**, author of *Expecting Wonder*

"If you need a voice of assurance, if you need a community of women who are not afraid of your dirty laundry, your struggles, your dreams, or your shame, you've found it. Reading Strong, Brave & Beautiful is like sitting with a circle of friends who get what it's like to be a mom. Not only will these essays make you feel less alone in the shake-your-head, want-to-crawl-in-a-hole, burst-your-heart-with-gratitude, ordinary days of motherhood, they will also remind you that you are already stronger, braver, and more beautiful than you know. Ready for a fresh dose of hope in your mothering? It's waiting for you on every page."

—**Becky Keife**, author of *No Better Mom for the Job* and community manager for (in)courage

"This honest collection of essays will be far more helpful and life-giving to new moms than any encyclopedia of baby and child care for those early years of mothering. The Kindred Mom team has written beautifully about the unforeseen challenges and revelations of motherhood—the uncertainty and joy that rises to the surface late at night in the rocker or in the wee hours of the morning waiting for a teenager to pull into the driveway. Mamas will relish the validation, relief, and kinship within these pages. Strong, Brave & Beautiful is a balm for the soul and a grace-filled gift for mamas clearing a path through the weeds of motherhood. I loved it."

—**Shauna Letellier**, author of *Remarkable Hope: When Jesus Revived Hope in Disappointed People*

"This book is a cool drink of Living Water for the mama who feels overwhelmed by the busyness, the messiness, the decision fatigue, and the thankless work of mothering. These essays include beautiful writing and honest truths about how to find strength and resilience on the journey of motherhood. I'm eager to share this with other mama friends who 'get it.'"

—**Dorina Lazo Gilmore-Young**, author of *Walk, Run, Soar* & *Cora Cooks Pancit*

"More than anything, moms long to be seen and known. In the pages of Strong, Brave & Beautiful, every mother will find herself in the powerful stories and compassionate understanding offered by the writers of this book. From poop disasters that make you laugh and groan with sympathy to the specific bittersweet of weaning to enthusiastic celebrations of not only surviving but thriving in an ordinary day, these essays paint vivid pictures of the highs and lows of parenting that will fill the hearts of mothers everywhere with camaraderie and encouragement. Read this book and know that you are not alone."

—**Meg Tietz**, author of *Spirit-Led Parenting* and host of *The Sorta Awesome Podcast*

# STRONG BRAVE & BEAUTIFUL

# STRONG BRAVE & BEAUTIFUL

## STORIES OF HOPE FOR MOMS IN THE WEEDS

EMILY SUE ALLEN

with managing editor
JENNIFER VAN WINKLE

*and writers from KindredMom.com*

ISBN 978-1-0879-0238-8 (PAPERBACK)
ISBN 978-1-0879-0239-5 (EPUB)

PUBLISHED BY KINDRED MOM
EMILY SUE ALLEN
6214 BOTHELL WAY NE
KENMORE, WA 98028
WWW.KINDREDMOM.COM

## BOOK CREDITS:

Concept
*Emily Sue Allen*

Managing Editor
*Jennifer Van Winkle*

Contributors
*Emily Sue Allen*
*Mary Kate Brown*
*Robin Chapman*
*Lindsey Cornett*
*Melissa Hogarty*
*Jacelya Jones*
*Bethany McMillon*
*Lynne Patti*
*Jennifer Van Winkle*

Proofreading Team
*Robin Chapman*
*Melissa Hogarty*
*K.C. Ireton*

Developmental Editing Team
*Emily Sue Allen*
*Mary Kate Brown*
*Lindsey Cornett*
*Bethany McMillon*
*Lynne Patti*

Cover & Interior Book Design
*Emily Sue Allen*

Book Launch Manger
*Mary Kate Brown*

Courageous Mamas:
We're cheering for you

# TABLE OF CONTENTS

# FOREWORD

*Adriel Booker*

I COULDN'T HAVE KNOWN OUR FAMILY WOULD HAVE FIVE people sick, three bouts of Covid testing, and (thankfully) eleven negative results over the time I read this manuscript. I didn't know how the unexpected would derail my "yes" or how my best laid plans to write a foreword for a project I deeply believe in would be disrupted.

A global pandemic changes things. No one has been untouched by 2020's interruptions, challenges, losses, and uncertainties. We can speculate how things will turn out, but one glance at the ever-changing news cycle reminds us that we don't even know what we don't know.

And isn't that a little like motherhood?

During my years as a mom, I've experienced loss that's devastated my sense of vision for the future. I've had to dig deep for creative ways to reinvent myself in roles I never consciously signed up for. I've been tired to the bone yet unable to sleep because my mind is full of all the things that feel unhinged. I've struggled to find purpose in the mundane and to dream or plan for the future when I feel overrun by the daily urgency of regular life. I've cried out to God for understanding and sometimes have been met with companionship instead of the concrete answers I was pleading for. I've had my values and priorities sifted and my resolve tested.

The pandemic has been hard for everyone, but those who are able to tap into their agility, resilience, creativity, and hopefulness are finding their way through the weeds anyway. We're learning to let the disruptions, the grief and loss, and the unforeseen challenges reveal things that need realigning in our lives, things that need reinforcing, and things that need reinventing. The pandemic is forcing us to let go, make sacrifices, look for small mercies, bounce back, and even receive gifts we never saw coming.

Becoming a mother has done this for me too.

Motherhood—the single most transformative mechanism for discipleship in my life to date. It's helped me see my great need for God's grace and the invaluable nature of my most precious relationships. It's fueled desperation to know who I am at the core of my being so I can love and lead well. And it's turned my life upside down, granting me perspective I couldn't have earned another way.

Using the pandemic as a metaphor for the disorienting experience of new motherhood is flawed (and I wonder how this will read when we've all come out on the "other side"), but I like to think we'll emerge more grounded, more confident to trust ourselves, more committed to one another's wellbeing, more sure about the things we value most, and more aware of the ways our lives are connected, less sidetracked by interruption, less likely to miss an unexpected opportunity, and more empathetic toward ourselves, our loved ones, and others. I hope we're more galvanized to discover clarity in the confusion and hope in the chaos, whatever form it takes next.

And isn't this what we also hope for when we find ourselves disarmed in those dizzying days of new motherhood?

The work of Emily Sue Allen and the Kindred Mom team has always been to provide a steady presence for moms who yearn for perspective to guide them during the most exhausting and transformative years of motherhood. They are cheerleaders and champions, but also friends and companions. They are the village we all wish we had, but sometimes lack. What the women in this collection of stories are about to show you is what I wish I knew when that first little boy was placed in my arms ten years ago:

*Strong* is not the opposite of weak. Strength is tenacity, resilience, vulnerability, saying, 'I was wrong, will you forgive me?' a hundred times, a willingness to ask for help, persevering gratitude, and the recognition of hope in moments of despair.

*Brave* is not the opposite of afraid. Brave means sharing the load, trusting our instincts, admitting "I don't know," saying the uncomfortable *no* to save room for the right *yes*, trying again when we fail, and forging ahead despite our doubts and unanswered questions.

*Beautiful* is not the opposite of messy. Beauty is being undone and remade in the image of our Creator. It is humility to confess our strengths when our weaknesses are much easier to articulate. It is the ongoing work of God's hand—the throughline of faithfulness to disciple us as we disciple those who come along behind us.

My work with bereaved families after pregnancy loss has helped me identify story as one of the most powerful currencies of grace—not transactional, but invitational. This is what you'll find in this collection: an invitation to embrace your own motherhood in both its grit and glory, its proudest moments and its most mundane.

As you read these stories, you will see glimpses of yourself through the tantrums, the Zoloft, the arguments, the laundry, the lullaby, the dirt, the Home Depot date nights. But I also hope you'll see what I see: the strength, bravery, and beauty of women committed to—as Lindsey writes—the "grace of confession." As you receive these confessions this is my prayer for you:

May you be inspired to move into the grace of your *own* confession. May you have eyes to see and name *your* strength, *your* bravery, *your* beauty. May you see that you're more than a mother—you're a woman shaped and formed in the image of our beautiful God. And may you see that yes, you're a woman who already mothers *well*.

I often tell my oldest, "We're growing up at the same time. I'm growing up as a mom while you're growing up as a young man—neither of us has more experience than the other as we grow into these roles." We're bound to display some immaturity, ignorance, selfishness, mistakes, even willful rebellion at times. But we're also bound to surprise ourselves with just how much capacity we hold inside for growth, for sacrificial love, for becoming all that God has designed us for. The stories in *Strong, Brave & Beautiful* remind us how much we've grown, that we *are* growing, and there is promise of growth ahead. The weeds cannot hold us.

Unlike Covid, we aren't hoping for a cure for motherhood. (Here's where the pandemic metaphor well and truly falls apart.) But we are hoping for this: to live as women in a world where we are interrupted, challenged, and even dismayed—at the mess and the noise and the sleepless nights (and your own fill-in-the-blank)—yet remain sure that we have what it takes to live and lead and love well despite having never done it before.

Here's to these "unprecedented times." Here's to doing it together. Here's to celebrating our stories while we're still in the middle. Here's to our Hope that keeps us tethered. Here's to knowing how strong, brave, and beautiful we are.

Adriel Booker
Author of *Grace Like Scarlett: Grieving with Hope after Miscarriage and Loss*
Sydney, Australia
August 2020

# INTRODUCTION

I WAS A YOUNG BRIDE. I made my wedding vows before friends and family just a month after my college graduation. It was a humble ceremony; a party to mark the official start of my independent adult life, and the first domino tipped into a long line of adventures to come my way alongside my sweetheart.

With all the maturity you would expect from a couple of kids just barely into their twenties, we planned to wait about five years before having children but left the door wide open with respect to contraception. It should be no surprise we became pregnant three months after the wedding.

The idea of becoming a mother had not seriously crossed my mind until the lines blinked at me. Or I blinked at them with a thrill and gasp and a resounding *yes* within me. *I embrace you, little one*, I wrote in my journal that day. At the end of my first term in grad school, I traded my intentions to study through seminary for a crash course in motherhood. I had much to learn—as in *everything*.

I had zero experience caring for an infant (or any small child), and the learning curve proved astronomical. Heart and eyes open wide with excitement and trepidation, I stepped into motherhood as green as they come.

Except for a week-by-week pregnancy book, I didn't read many books prior to the birth of my first daughter. I watched a few birth story shows on TLC, but with my focus on the big event, I didn't give much thought to all the stuff beyond her arrival. One domino crashed into another, and thus began years of wild adventures raising my sweet girl and the six other children who came after her.

For me, motherhood came more suddenly than naturally. With new stages and challenges arriving all the time, I quickly learned just how much I didn't know. I bumbled through all kinds of baby and toddler nonsense, and as our family grew, I searched desperately for a guide, for the right answers to my pressing motherhood questions. I felt unsure of myself, doubted my ability to raise a child without falling on my face a hundred times. I unearthed new, vulnerable caverns in my soul. I started asking lots of questions.

*Who am I now that my life is a messy collection of crumbs and perpetual exhaustion?*

*Am I cut out for life with toddlers? With teenagers?*

*How will our marriage survive the onslaught of demands we both feel weighing heavily on us?*

*How will I know what to do when we hit new challenges?*

*Will I ever get used to these stretch marks, this body that has been forever changed in the process of nurturing children?*

Fourteen years have passed since that humble season of discovery. I'm still painfully aware of how much I have yet to learn regarding what my children need from me at each turn, and I still bumble through the new ages and stages we are leaning into as a family, but I have also observed some very important things.

Motherhood is a painful, constant lesson in staying the course, learning to depend on God, troubleshooting major and minor problems in the same hour (every hour, some days), and wading through big feelings to cultivate grit, courage, and resilience.

Mothers are a powerful, beautiful force of love in an increasingly broken world.

Mothers are strong in ways not always easily seen on the outside.

Mothers face and conquer fears from the earliest weeks of gestation through the launch of their grown kids into the world (and I would imagine beyond, but I'm not there yet).

This collection of essays is a modest offering—reflections on the humble and holy moments we've experienced as women who celebrate the value of life, the treasure of home, and the beauty of learning how to care for children, care for our marriages, and care for ourselves.

We hope you see parts of your own story woven through ours and recognize that you, too, are Strong, Brave, and Beautiful.

*Emily Sue Allen*
Founder of KindredMom.com

PART I

# WHEN RESILIENCE FEELS LIKE FLOUNDERING

*Emily Sue Allen*

I'VE GOT A KID ON MY HIP, a 3-year-old melting down at my feet, and four other children squawking and wailing their way through the day. My hands are full, and my house is a bonafide mess. I'd love to invite friends over, but I quickly shove that idea to the back burner where my shame is cooking on low.

Dirty clothes litter the floor, clean clothes are piled on my bed, and a fresh load needs rescuing from the dryer so I can put clean pajamas on these kids before I put them to bed for the night. I gather the warm garments in my arms and transport the oversized load from the dryer to my bedroom across the hall. A haphazard trail of dropped socks ends at a mountain of clean laundry.

There are clothes everywhere. Crumbs everywhere. Children everywhere.

No matter how hard I try to pull everything together, to clean all the messes and neatly stow our stuff out of sight, it never stays like that.

I sweep, vacuum, Swiffer, and steam. I gather, straighten, and organize. I inhale, hold my breath for ten seconds, and exhale only to discover new crumbs have magically appeared and new bins have been overturned. With every jaunt through a room to pick up toys, I grow more and more resentful until I am not placing, but emphatically throwing toys into their bins. Crash, bang, boom. I sputter unkind commands at my wide-eyed children, while the gross feeling of constantly missing the mark as a home manager hangs on me—along with all the tasks never completed in a final and satisfying manner. The mess of my home is a tidal wave, the impetus of a shame spiral, and I am floundering through it.

Well-meaning mamas a few steps ahead have told me I need to get my kids involved with household chores. I hear the advice, but I also spy an unfortunate, enormous chasm between my kids' current cleaning proficiency and where they need to be to help in a meaningful way. I don't know how to get from here to there.

I struggle to see the beauty in my days, to see any beauty or strength within me. All I see is mess, mess, overwhelm, and mess. I feel like I just can't get it right, like maybe I'm not cut out for this. I feel like a failure.

I want my kids to understand they are capable of hard work, to know some things will require us to dig in and do what is needed even when we fear we'll never get it right.

If I want them to believe they can work hard, I have to show them how by doing it myself. The mothering years are hard, but they are also pregnant with joy, full of wonder and discovery, and these hidden treasures are discovered and appreciated precisely through the challenges we encounter and overcome.

The truth is, I am working out resilience in real time. I am strengthened and I gain experience to navigate my *next* disaster in the midst of every challenge I work through.

Taking small, faithful steps toward doing what needs to be done—*without* a furrowed brow and a negative attitude—is the best way to combat the voice of shame. Resilience often feels like floundering, but really, it is about movement. Resilience is about recognizing the power I have to move in a new direction: from standing still in a place of struggle to finding the courage to take just one step forward. It is not about results, and it doesn't hinge on the words *successful, fulfilled, strong,* and *in control.* Resilience is about rising to each challenge, engaging my responsibilities, and growing in flexibility and strength while I learn to navigate new seas.

Discouragement is not meant to be a destination but is a momentary acknowledgment that where I am is not where I want to be.

The truth is, the tasks that never seem complete are not an indictment of my inability to stay ahead of the mess. Instead, they remind me that a meaningful life must be tended day in and day out. My laundry pile serves as an opportunity to recognize the beauty of these messy years and to cultivate resilience as I return to this humble task again and again.

The active, physical labor of keeping a home is necessary, meaningful work. The best thing I can do is silence shame and chip away at my laundry pile, one pair of socks and one pair of pants at a time. This *is* resilience.

# WHAT NOW?

*Melissa Hogarty*

W HEN WE BROUGHT OUR LITTLE ORANGE BABY
home from the hospital, we set him down next
to the piano, asleep in his car seat, and looked at each other.
*What now?*

*How on earth were we supposed to take care of a baby...*
*by ourselves?*

His entire life so far, I felt like we were being graded.
Everyone who stepped into our room on the maternity ward
kindly explained I knew nothing and urged me to keep a
detailed log of his schedule. I assumed something terrible
would happen if I neglected this—if I couldn't answer their
inquiries clearly. Nurses came at all hours to discuss my son's
weight, his pooping habits, and how his circumcision was
healing.

When we arrived home with our baby, I wasn't sure
what came next—I felt unqualified to handle a newborn
independently. My son wasn't latching well, and no nurses
hovered nearby to grab my boob and show me a different

hold that might work. Help was gone.

We were alone.

*What now?*

My husband and I looked with bewilderment around our living room and then down at the sleeping, jaundiced baby who was about to turn our lives completely upside down. We felt like imposters. What were we supposed to do with this little person? Were we allowed to leave him in the car seat as he slept? Would someone jump out of the curtains and scold us if we tucked him into a Boppy on the couch?

After a short discussion, we dragged the car seat next to the window so the sun could shine down and change his face into a less startling color. As all our blurred snapshots would later show, he looked alarmingly like someone had dipped him into a bucket of apricot dye.

Our first visit to the pediatrician was scheduled for the following day, and I already had a pit in my stomach—like I'd neglected to study for the most important exam of the year. I worried they would readmit him to the hospital for phototherapy. I didn't know yet that the doctor would need me to strip my child naked to assess him properly. The next afternoon, we would show up at the pediatrician's office with a bulging diaper bag, a baby comfortably dressed in short sleeves, and no blanket. We would miss our appointment window (because we had no idea how to leave the house with a newborn) and subsequently find ourselves shivering in a freezing supply closet (the only place our pediatrician could work us in), trying to wrap our son in a burp cloth and shield his naked body with our arms. If shame literally burned, I could have kept that room toasty with the heat of all the things I wished I had known earlier. In that moment, jaundice would barely register on my emotional radar.

But I couldn't see any of this yet. The first day in our living room, I was too busy fretting about being in charge of someone else's life, realizing that all those years of babysitting had not prepared me after all.

When he awoke, I sat down on the couch to nurse him, half-buried in a mountain of pillows. I couldn't tell if I was feeding him correctly, but it sure hurt like the dickens and made a slippery mess. My husband sat next to me, leaning into the mountain, holding our son's tiny fists away from his face. We whispered little jokes to him to mask our growing frustration. "Fingers are friends, not food."

I cried as he struggled to latch. His problem was not a dreaded tongue tie, but that after spending six hours being squeezed in my birth canal, all he wanted to do was bite. And boy, did he. He suffered from a clamp-down reflex so ferocious that we later nicknamed him "Tiger Baby." Never have I been so grateful God made newborns toothless.

When mealtime was as finished as it was going to get, we looked out the window at the sunny skies and decided to go for a walk. We tucked our baby into his bright red stroller and set out on a slow neighborhood circuit. Three doors down, a pregnant neighbor ran out to meet us. She cooed over our tiny son and handed us a congratulatory bottle of wine. We stuck it in the basket beneath the baby seat and kept walking.

Precisely halfway around the block, when turning back would take just as long as pressing forward, I discovered that I could not walk any farther. This had never happened to me before. I was mistress of my body, always. If I said go, it went. I might move slowly, but I never quit. *How could I hit my limit after less than half a mile?*

My husband graciously offered to get the car, but I couldn't admit that level of defeat. Instead, I took a small step forward every five seconds. The throbbing, wounded space between my legs felt like it was about to fall out of my body onto the sidewalk. Sitting down would be a dream. Preferably with ice.

When we finally made it back home, I stood gingerly on our lawn with the baby while my husband folded our stroller. The forgotten bottle of wine crashed onto the concrete driveway and shattered.

A little something shattered inside my heart too. Somehow, that bottle of wine represented my independence. It meant I could still relax and enjoy something that had nothing to do with a hungry, pumpkin-faced baby. Its demise felt like an existential loss I could never recoup. My hope for relief was running down the driveway in dark, red rivulets.

It would be weeks before I got over the feeling that my life as a mother was one big test. It would be weeks before I discovered the joy of having my baby curl his body toward mine, reaching for me because, to him, I was the world.

It would be months before I began to trust my intuition more than the advice of strangers.

It would be years before I accepted the truth: sometimes I will get it wrong, but my mettle is measured by my *next* effort. Will I give up when I blunder, or will I choose to go boldly forward, trusting God's grace to cover over my mistakes?

God has called me into motherhood, and He is the one who defines me. I'm not a bad mother if I don't predict the need for extra blankets or two changes of clothes. Yes, it's uncomfortable to make mistakes because I don't know what to expect. Yes, I still wish for the certainty of knowing what will come next.

But now I realize I could see just enough that first day. His little tongue sticking out. His little orange fists and dark hair. His trust. His love. And mine.

# THE MAKING OF A MAMA

*Mary Kate Brown*

THE MOMENT SHE WAS BORN, I was born. In those final moments of labor when I was pushing—surrounded by nurses, legs warm and heavy from anesthesia, bright lights in my face—I realized this was it. She was coming. This moment was the threshold between the life I was familiar with and the one I had longed to live for years. Suddenly, she was in my arms, on my chest, squinty-eyed and grappling for some familiarity in her bright new world. Suddenly, there I was: *Mama*. Beholding the very one who made me so.

She was new, and so was I; we both had things to learn. I sat uncomfortably in my hospital bed, dutifully attending to an endless cycle of syringe-feeding, nursing, expressing, and pumping. Patiently and stubbornly, I struggled through the pain of a sore back and postpartum cramping while learning how to nurse my baby who could not yet latch. I began to understand the cost of becoming someone's mama. For nine months, her body relied on me for life, and she'd continue to do so for many more.

Upon going home a few short days later, we were surrounded by countless faces. Visitors brought gifts and meals, all eager for baby snuggles. I looked forward to the end of our days when it would be just us again. In the middle of those quiet nights, she and I sat on our living room couch beneath dim lights. Nobody told me my body would feel as though it barely survived a round in a boxing ring. Nobody told me my back would bear the brunt of my lack of nursing experience. Nobody told me stitches would make sitting down comfortably impossible. Nobody told me how I might cry and cry and cry because the beauty of the life I birthed would be so overwhelming. An unfathomable depth of love came pouring out in heavy, silent sobs in the still hours of those nights.

Though sleep-deprived, I couldn't sleep because I didn't want to miss a moment of her. Though healing from birth, I was already anticipating how I could protect her heart from hurt. Though struggling with my own postpartum pains and struggles, I was stubbornly concerned about whether or not she was eating enough.

Though I was a grown, adult woman with a child of her own, suddenly I was a brand new person. I was someone's mama, trying to get up on my own two feet and solely motivated by love. At no other time did this reality weigh on me so heavily as in those early weeks following the birth of my first child. After she came into our lives, each day brought new firsts. My husband and I lived for each moment, completely enamored simply by who she was. She was beautiful. Every breath was wonder-filled. Every sleepy grin was awe-worthy. Every small stir was attention-grabbing.

And there I was: a love-struck, messy-haired,

sleep-deprived, pajama-wearing, milk-and-spit-up-covered amateur mama. I didn't realize it at the time, but alongside all those unglamorous things, I was becoming something wonderful. I was growing deeper, more multifaceted, more aware of my resilience and strength. I grew keenly aware of this capacity to love the life of another so fiercely.

In the nine months I carried her, I had been a mother. Her birth ushered in a new iteration, a new phase in my burgeoning motherhood journey. As my wearied body pushed her body into the world, I was also pushed into a new sphere of life. Becoming a mama was all at once messy and overwhelming, while filled with moments of surprising beauty. In an unexpected way, I found I was somehow myself *and* someone new at the very same time.

I birthed her, but she made me.

# SPEED BOAT/OCEAN LINER

*Jennifer Van Winkle*

*She once had a little speed boat she traded in for an ocean liner. Some days, she really missed how that little boat could skip along like a rock on a still pond, but she fell in love with the people she met on board that great big ship. She figured regardless of the boat she was sailing on, she was still out on the water, and that was freedom.*

FOR A FRACTION OF A MOMENT, I considered flopping down on the couch to close my eyes. The beginning of parenthood with twin infants had been all about survival for my husband and me. This afternoon, my eyes burned, my heart fluttered, and all I desired was one moment to myself. The house was quiet. The twins were asleep, and my husband had returned to work. "Sleep when your babies sleep." I didn't have that luxury because my milk was in high demand and in short supply. I had standing dates with the breast pump every hour. *I wonder if there is a way to do this and sleep at the same time,* I thought. Sleeping and pumping don't mix—I shed many tears over spilt milk.

*The schedule says it's time to feed them.*

*But they're not crying...they aren't even awake.*

*Maybe I should let them sleep.*

*"Let sleeping dogs lie," right? Let sleeping babies sleep?*

*Maybe for a little while...the doctors said I need to wake them to feed. They need to grow.*

I woke, diapered, and placed each baby consecutively into individual bouncer chairs. My heavy body groaned as I walked to the kitchen to prepare their bottles—part breastmilk, part formula. Opening the top to the bottle warmer, a flash of envy hit my mind. My tiny sliver of personal time slipped away with each escalating cry. We were all remembering, my babies and I: they remembered their hunger, I remembered a past life.

*Remember what it felt like to be a normal human being?*

*...Coming and going as I pleased?*

*That seems like such a long time ago.*

*I wonder if I'll ever have that kind of freedom again?*

I made the first bottle a little hot on purpose, so it would have time to cool off by the time the second bottle finished warming.

*I am so tired; I just want to go to sleep.*

*Sometimes I wonder if having kids was such a good idea.*

*It is so much harder than I thought.*

I needed my body to be in top physical form, but it desperately needed healing from the ordeal of gestating and birthing two baby boys within 11 minutes of each other. My boys were born six weeks early, and for three weeks they were hospitalized in the NICU. My brand-new mama-heart heavily doubted my ability to care for them. Wires and monitors tangled across their bodies made it difficult to act on my maternal instincts to hold them close.

*What parent in their right mind could leave their precious babies alone in a strange place with strange people and go home and sleep in their own bed at night?*

Little did I know the doubt that developed in those first weeks would be the impetus for a positive change later on.

The beginning of my motherhood journey was tumultuous, and as the four walls of my home closed in, I was frantic for something to give.

*Enough is enough. I'm not going to hold myself prisoner in my own house.*

I began to summon all my courage to get out of the house by myself with my two tiny babies, even though it would have been entirely easier to stay home and wait for the coveted help of my husband. I exchanged the spontaneity I once enjoyed for preparedness. My bottom line became, "Do what you can to set your family up for success." Every endeavor came on the heels of tactical planning, envisioning every conceivable scenario I would encounter, and making sure to have a plan and supplies in place.

I lumbered out the front door with a bucket-style infant car seat in the crook of each arm and a diaper bag slung across my back. The balance made it easier than carrying one at a time. The three of us must have looked crazy taking up so much space, but my desire for independence trumped my need to blend in.

I finally found the nerve to drive downtown to introduce my new sons to some work colleagues. The whole way, I mentally rehearsed the steps to get them from the car into the building.

*First I'm going to get the baby from the seat behind me.*

*Then I'll go around and get the other one.*

*Yeah, that makes sense because my diaper bag is on that side of the car.*

I got the boys successfully out of the car, looped my arms through the twin car seat handles like the pro I was becoming, and called the front desk to let them know we'd arrived.

My friend greeted me outside the building just before we reached the front door. She tried to go in for a hug as is natural, but awkwardly stopped short because there was no way I could hug her back.

"It is so good to see you," she said.

I smiled the biggest I had in a long time. I smiled because I loved seeing a friend, but mostly because my heart was soaring.

*I am actually doing it—I'm out of the house with the babies for the first time!*

A few days ago, a dear friend described how fractured and confining her life felt as she tried to juggle a professional life, motherhood, and her own personal desires. The balancing act sounded familiar to me, especially when she lamented about how doing anything with a young child requires an insane amount of planning. An arrow straight to my heart.

My life before children was much like that agile little speed boat. I was fortunate to have the freedom to do pretty much anything I wanted when I wanted. Want to go out to the pub for dinner? Sure. Itching to hit the road? No problem—saddle up, partner. Those days were pretty footloose and are a stark contrast to life with children. However, I never wish for my life to be the way it was before children…

unless I am trying to go to the bathroom.

Life with children is like the ocean liner—it equally carries tons of responsibility and wonder. It is an island oasis in the midst of an unforgiving environment, and it can't corner for crap.

Preparedness brought balance to those early days of motherhood. I emerged from those first survival-ridden days with confidence that I can handle anything coming my way.

I am an ocean-liner mother, and I am also that footloose young woman with her speed boat. The spontaneity of my youth gave birth to my adventurous heart. The experience of having children required preparedness so they can one day develop that same taste for adventure.

Maybe you are a mama who is missing her speed boat. Maybe you wonder if it is possible to still be that young woman—the one who wore the flirtatious fragrance of spontaneity, even though, as a mom, your fragrance is more Eau de Spit-Up. Who says there are no surprises on an ocean liner, no magic in the steady forward momentum of a mama still chasing adventure while her little ones are along for the ride?

You have traded speed and agility for endurance and strength. Your ocean liner is built to handle adversity while providing comfort for all aboard, and you can go farther into the vast sea than that little speed boat ever dreamed of. The woman you once were is still you; she will always be you. More souls have come aboard, but you are still the captain of your ship, and you are still sailing.

# SERIOUSLY EVERYWHERE

*Robin Chapman*

THERE IS POOP SERIOUSLY EVERYWHERE, and I need to figure out what to do. I look around for an adultier adult—but of course, my husband is at work and the second-best candidate for "adult" is 6 years old, so there is only me. Me, on not nearly enough sleep, with a screaming 6-month-old and my dominant hand in a non-removable, absorbent cast as a result of recent surgery.

*Fan-freaking-tastic.*

I'm at a complete loss in the bathroom, my right arm in the air and my left hand trying valiantly to clean up the unbelievable mess of toddler excrement. My 6-year-old is helpfully trying to keep the baby happy, and my 4-year-old is less-helpfully stealing my phone and ferreting it away under her bed. My 2-year-old boy with the sad brown eyes is crying because he has poop all over him, and I feel very much alone.

Life as a stay-at-home mama to four is often a solitary and unwitnessed experience. I make a million small decisions, mediate a million small (or large) disagreements, answer a million pressing questions, all before lunch. Most of the work I do is invisible. Laundry gets folded, then dirty again. Dishes are used as soon as they're clean. Toddlers need the same limits enforced over…and over…and over again. And between all these things, the baby needs to be fed. Basically nothing I do stays done for very long. It's a good life. It's the one I dreamed of 30 years ago, when I was a bit younger than my oldest is now. But still, it's lonely and invisible sometimes.

Except it isn't. Through all of that, there is One who is with me. Emmanuel. He sees.

I am not alone.

I remember this in the chaos. Rather, He taps my shoulder to remind me He is *present*. Emmanuel.

I cry out to Him. I leave the bathroom for a second with all the noise and my arm still over my head and holler, "Jesus! I HAVE NO IDEA WHAT TO DO HERE!"

He is here. More than that, to my great relief, He has an answer. Not an all-encompassing Big Answer like He sometimes gives. Nobody walks through my door with hands to help, and I don't have a new game plan for handling today's crazy, but I suddenly know the next thing to do: *get rid of the jammies.*

I bring a plastic grocery sack to the bathroom, strip the boy, put the jammies in the bag and *throw them away.* Then I go back out to the living room and holler again. (I realize Emmanuel is *with me*, even—sometimes especially—in the bathroom, but my poor boy is already freaking out and I don't want to alarm him further.)

"OKAY, JESUS! NOW WHAT?!?"

And on we go. One step at a time, with noise and mess and absolute entropy, I live out this crazy poop-filled morning, knowing God is truly with me.

I am the oldest of five. Two of my siblings live near me in Alaska and two live elsewhere. The oldest of my little sisters lives on the other side of the world. She moved there a few years ago to follow the call of this God who is with *her.* The trouble? We only became actual, soul-deep friends a handful of years before that. All through our growing up years, there was competition and antagonism. Finally in our twenties (a surprise gift from the Giver of all good things!), our hearts connected with a depth I never anticipated. And now she lives in a place that is ten hours ahead of me, so nearly halfway around the world.

We can talk frequently because living in the future is magical—rather than waiting weeks for letters to go back and forth across continents and oceans (if they arrive at all), we can send messages instantly, even talk in real time. We know what is happening in each other's lives and with each other's kids. I see pictures of her toddler who has springy curls nearly identical to the ones my oldest sported at that age. I see the baby who is just a couple months ahead of my youngest.

It's almost the same as if she were here.

But I miss her company. She is not *with* me.

There's no hanging out on my futon, drinking tea while discussing everything and nothing, interrupted more than once a minute by our collective seven children. No impromptu playdates at the park or McDonalds. We talk. She knows a lot of little bits of my life—poop shenanigans and all. We understand each other. But we don't have the chance right now to do life together.

I want her in my actual life, even though I know she can't be. But God *is* this kind of present. He doesn't just know about me; He is here.

Emmanuel. *God with us.* I can't see Him, so sometimes it feels like He's absent—on the other side of the globe. But He is here, seriously everywhere, in the day-to-day, mundane, boring details. He sees. He is with me, and not bound by distance or time zones. This name, usually relegated to the Nativity story, is a lifeline.


That morning with the poop and the cast and the screaming toddlers and the jammies in the trash was eventually fine. At the end of it all, everything was clean, including that cast I needed to wear for another several days. The children were fed. Laundry was started and books were read. What I most needed that morning was Someone with me, both guiding and bearing witness to it all. I needed company, not in an abstract "exchange details of the day from a distance" way like I do with my sister, but in a "hang out in the mess" kind of way.

I needed Emmanuel. And the same Emmanuel who came through all the mess of birth into all the mess of our world did not disappoint.

He never does.

# STRUGGLE VS. FAILURE

*Lindsey Cornett*

I T WAS LEO'S FIRST BIRTHDAY, and I was sobbing into my steering wheel. Back at the house, my mother-in-law waited with our two sons and a tray of lion-shaped birthday cookies she had made. I had come to pick up my husband from work so he could join us back at home for the celebration. In the backseat were a Mylar balloon and a smash cake, which I had picked up hastily from the grocery store just minutes before.

*I can't do this anymore. I can't do this anymore. I can't do this anymore.* The thought raged and roared. When Evan opened the car door, he caught one glimpse of my wet and splotchy cheeks, and his eyes widened with concern.

I had recognized my anxiety some months before, after listening to a podcast episode in which the hosts shared their own experiences with mental illness. I stopped short in my kitchen that day, listening to the sound of the humming dishwasher and those two women sharing vulnerably. I recognized myself in their stories. When I

51

found myself unexpectedly pregnant that spring, with Leo only 3 months old and Ian stuck in the terrible twos, I recognized the monumental weight of all I was facing and confessed this anxiety to my doctor. But at the time, I convinced myself I had everything under control. More prayer and more time away from the kids should take care of it, I thought.

As my womb swelled with the growth of my daughter and we walked from winter into spring and summer, I found no relief. In the weeks surrounding Leo's November birthday, I canceled appointments and kept my oldest home from preschool for no other reason than it felt impossible to leave the house.

When I watched Leo dip his finger into the white buttercream frosting of his first birthday cake, I was afraid.

I didn't fear the labor or delivery of our daughter in January, nor did I fear the coming reality of having two babies only 14 months apart. I was afraid of my own emotions, my own mind, and my own capability or lack thereof. I didn't know if I could survive parenting a third child.

I was full of excuses for how I was feeling. We had moved across the country, 1,200 miles away from our family and friends. Evan worked long hours, and we didn't have much support. Our oldest son, Ian, presented a slew of behavioral challenges. We struggled under the weight of student loan payments. Always a perfectionist, I blamed myself for any less-than-ideal day (which was basically all of them, with two children under 3 years old). My postpartum hormones never had a chance to return to normal before my third pregnancy complicated things even further.

It turned out, what I labeled "excuses" were actually risk factors.

My nurse and doctor went through the typical rigama-role—arm cuff and blood pressure, scale and weight, blue goop and baby's heartbeat, syringe and bloodwork. At one point, my doctor remarked on how very close this next delivery would be to my last.

"Everything looks good," she offered. "Any questions for me?"

"Well, there is one thing I need to ask you about."

She stood at the side of the exam table and held my hand as I wept, leaving only to retrieve another tissue from the box near the sink. I explained how I had been feeling: the racing heartbeat and itchy neck, the inability to catch my breath, the looping thoughts and strange fears.

I stand in the kitchen while the boys play in the living room. I can feel my heartbeat all the way up in my throat instead of deep in my chest, and I wonder if I am having a heart attack. I start to itch all over my body.

I lie in bed early in the morning, and I can hear the baby stirring in his nursery across the hall. I pull the duvet all the way up over my head. When Evan comes in to ask what I'm doing, I say I have a headache, but actually I am hoping to disappear.

I hold a laundry basket on my hip at the top of the basement stairs and look down. The light is on and the railing is secure and the basket is not too heavy, but in my mind's eye, I watch myself trip and tumble down the stairs, again and again, baby onesies flying through the air.

I left the OBGYN that day with a clean bill of health for our growing third child and a Zoloft prescription scrawled on a white slip of paper.

In late December, a few weeks after beginning my medication, I snuck into Leo's nursery while he slept.

I stood over his crib, trying to keep my feet still, lest the creaky floor wake him. Suddenly I saw him, as though for the first time. I ran to grab my camera because I wanted to remember this moment—the sweetness of face, the roundness of his cheeks, and the depth of my previously dormant devotion—forever.

The next day at breakfast, I sat down at the kitchen table. Ian ate Cheerios in his seat, and Leo clumsily tried to spoon oatmeal into his mouth. Just a few weeks before, I spent every breakfast hiding in the kitchen, wishing to go back to bed and looking ahead at the day with dread. But on this day, I sat down at the table without thinking about it. I laughed with my boys, sipped my Earl Grey, and felt Ruthie kicking in my belly. I smiled.


A few weeks after Ruthie was born, Leo fell off the changing table. It happened exactly like they always say: "It only takes a second." Ruthie was crying in the crib behind me, so I turned to pop her pacifier back into her mouth. I looked back as little Leo was flipping over the table's edge. I can still hear myself yelling his name.

The nurse on the phone worked hard to get my attention. "Hey, Mama?" she said, "Listen to me. These things happen. Okay? These things happen all the time. Everything is going to be fine. Babies are resilient."

When things calmed and it was clear Leo was unscathed, I said to Evan, "I feel like I've been failing at being Leo's mom since the moment he was born."

Until I said that word aloud—*failure*—I hadn't realized I'd pinned the label to myself. I could feel it like a thorny vine, tripping me up. The word had wrapped its tendrils around my heart and was squeezing the life out of my motherhood.

Some moments in life function like hinges on a door: this is the juncture from which everything will swing one way or the other. Leo's fall from the changing table was one such moment. I could either look at it as confirmation that I was, indeed, a failure, or I could accept the grace Jesus offered me. My identity was not "good mom," "happy mom," or "perfect mom," but simply "beloved child of God." If God's grace was big enough to cover my pride and selfishness, my dishonesty and anger, my addictions and fears, then it was certainly big enough to cover my motherhood.

Evan looked at me through the dark of our bedroom and reminded me of the same things the nurse had said on the phone: Leo was resilient and doing just fine. I was a good mom and not at all a failure.

Somehow, for the first time since Leo's birth, I began to believe it.

I am a good mom. I am not a failure.

Healing from postpartum depression involves grief. I mourn the year I lost and the uncomfortable reality that I was unwell. My limited understanding of postpartum depression clouded my vision at the time. I didn't have suicidal thoughts and was managing to care for my kids, so I assumed I was fine. Now I know better. I sometimes ask myself, *would I have ever sought help for my PPD had my new pregnancy not necessitated a fresh batch of prenatal appointments, if I hadn't been so alarmed by my fear, and if that podcast episode hadn't given me language to articulate my confusing mental state?*

Looking back, I remember very little from Leo's first year of life. I look at photos, but the memories escape me.

I loved that little boy, but I could not connect with him. I was terrified to say so out loud, believing it would be the thing that solidified my standing as a terrible mother.

Still, confession is powerful. While the medication was healing the imbalance in my brain, my heart did not begin to recover until the moment I acknowledged these struggles out loud. The grace of confession helped me challenge the lies about my capability as a mother, lies about the well-being of my children, and the lie that my value exists in keeping it all together.

Leo's fall did not make me a failure, nor did postpartum depression. To "succeed" as a parent (if we can even measure parenting in terms of successes and failures, which I doubt), we must live, work, and care for our children with courage in the midst of shortcomings and difficulties. I loved and parented my kids as best I could while battling depression and anxiety. I asked for help the moment I was able to.

In motherhood—as in the rest of life—the space between "struggle" and "failure" is vast.

# PART II

# FILTH

*Lynne Patti*

THE SHARP YELLING REVERBERATES OFF THE BATHROOM walls. Between outbursts, my son's face is set like steel. I wonder if the neighbors can hear him, the rage spilling out of him. I ask him calmly and quietly to wash his feet in the running water.

Moving out of the city and into the country just under two years ago was the best decision we have ever made. Our sprawling backyard invites our five children to run, explore, and get dirty. They play hard all day, and at bedtime, muddy feet tread sleepily upstairs to get ready for bed.

On this particular evening, my 8-year-old son makes his way to the sink to brush his teeth in his jammies. My keen mama-eyes spy little brown circles left behind from the Crocs he wore all day in the backyard. The tiny spots on his little boy feet are immortalized in backyard grime even though his shoes were discarded downstairs a while ago. Dirt and sweat harmonize into round dots telling the story of his country adventures.

I look closer and follow the filth as it trails up his calf, winds around his shin, and ends with dramatic dirt splotches around his knee. I simultaneously think, *Wow. What a fun day he had!* and *We've gotta get that cleaned off before he slips into his sheets.*

I casually say, "Lukey, let's get you in the bath to get your legs and feet cleaned off."

And so begins the crescendo.

As I bend to wash the filth from his lower extremities, he spits filth out of his mouth. He screams at me, resists, and lashes out physically. He yells that he hates me and his whole family—venom to my mama-heart. He laments ever having been chosen to be in this family. "Why are you so mean?" is a common refrain as well, delivered so heartily that it booms through the halls of our home—*fortissimo.* I calmly count down from five (our most-used disciplinary tactic, preventing indefinite stalls) after each command I give him. "Put your foot under the water. Five, four, three, two, one. Give me the other foot. Five, four, three, two, one. Carefully step out of the tub. Five, four, three, two, one." My calm assertions are the elevator music to his death metal.

He continues to kick and spout. Three years ago, if one of my children behaved this way, I would have been knocked out for days. I would have fretted about everything I've done wrong as a mother and then brainstormed all the systems I would put in place to make. it. stop. But I've learned. I have learned that in this storm, his storm, there's only one option. I've been here so many times before and I know I must press on. It's the only way. I must finish the seemingly simple task at hand (tonight, removing the tiny brown circles and splotches with soap and water) and then sit down to debrief. Enduring the raging, ranting, bitter storm is how I travel all the way down to his heart.

In moments like these, I have learned my son challenges me so viciously because he wants to know if I'll go all the way to Hell and back with him. He seeks my loyalty even when he displays his darkest side. Will I stay? Will I love him even if he dares to let me see what's really pulsing underneath his cool-guy exterior? Will I tend to his filth whether it comes on feet too big for his body or from the core of his heart? Will I bend to signal that I'm there for him, supporting him, undergirding him?

The answer is yes. Yes, I will.

The tirade ebbs, and with clean, dry feet and legs, he dives head-first into his bed. I begin to rub his back and I see the resistance begin to diminish.

"Buddy, look at me."

"No." I feel his whole body slightly tense again, but I know the roaring climax of his symphony has given way to softer tones. It's quieter now.

"I love you no matter what. I am here for you. Is there something that happened today that you want to tell me?" I wait, his face still buried. Patience is absolutely essential in these moments. The seconds seem like hours as I wait for his response.

Head down, tears flowing, eyes averted, he lets it all out. The earlier string of vitriol spouted out in staccatos in the bathtub is replaced with a tearful stream of mumbles and moans, offenses and confusion. It's a cadenza only a mother could translate. I know exactly what he's saying:

*"A friend, a brother, a sister, did this and that and something else, and I didn't like it and it made me feel less-than and I felt stupid and I didn't know what to do or where to run and I*

*didn't have time to process any of it until you asked me to wash my feet, and somehow that made me explode and I couldn't help but unleash everything on you because I trust you and I know you will be here for all of it and I need that assurance from you because you're my safe place."*

There's always a rhythm.

Rage, resist, recoil.

Respond, release, restore.

It's only the bending to wash the filth away after the rage-resist-recoil pattern that ushers the response-release-restoration into being. I know this well because I have a Savior who bent over my filth and ushered me into restoration, washing me even though I raged and resisted and recoiled from His love. It's a cadence my son knows intuitively because he resembles me, a line from the same score—different, yet complementary.

I lift his exhausted body to mine and we snuggle upright together in his little-boy bed. As I press on toward the challenges of motherhood still ahead of me, I will replay this musical masterpiece of raging crescendos, staccato choruses, and gentler refrains. By the end I will know it by heart. I hold all of him now, physically wrapped up in my arms, surrendered and supported. I can do that because he trusts me to hold all of him emotionally first. He hugs back with all his might. He finally shows me his face and I notice the crying has stopped.

"I love you, Mommy."

Restoration resounds and the filth is forgiven.

# POOP MOUNTAIN

*Jennifer Van Winkle*

M Y NERVES ARE SHOT. Perhaps it is because my toddler's new favorite place to play is on top of the dining room table, or because the twins have mastered the art of overshooting the toilet. Whatever the reason, I need to get the whole crew outside *pronto* if I have a prayer of preserving what sanity I have remaining. The winter sun is making a rare appearance today, but here in Seattle, rain is never far away. I enjoy the cheerful warmth on my skin and smile even though, moments ago, I finished cleaning pee off the bathroom wall for the fourth time this week. I cram my toddler into a full-body rain suit (because I have weather-related trust issues), and lovingly remind my preschoolers to put on their rain boots for the 80 millionth time, perhaps with a little too much urgency (read: impatience).

Our Costco folding wagon, the designer handbag of mothers with multiple children, is loaded down with approximately 80 pounds of happy kids. I grab the handle and lumber down the busy street to the nature trails at the end of the block. Momentum and a slight downward grade make the load a little easier—every step a little closer to peace and farther from the chaos of my house.

At the trailhead, the children jump out of the wagon and eagerly scamper down the gravel path amid trees, ferns, and singing birds. The whole scene is entirely saccharine and idyllic, and I breathe relief, relishing one peaceful moment. My boys announce they want to hike a few hundred yards farther to climb Gravel Mountain, a term they coined when they were 2 years old for a sad rock pile measuring two feet high at best. Cheap entertainment. They march down the trail like soldiers; their little sister and I bring up the rear. Little Sis is excited to walk on her own two feet—without my help—just like her big brothers.

Volunteers recently worked to improve the trail network, evidenced by sections of fresh gravel and drainage rock in the places prone to flooding during heavy rains. On our way to Gravel Mountain, a large pile of fist-sized drainage rock blocks the trail. Wide-eyed, as if they just spied the Paw Patrol display at Toys"R"Us for the first time, the boys race ahead to scramble over the new obstacle.

It is a happily-ever-after picture of all things rosy and bright. My daughter toddles along behind her brothers. My two boys stand at the top of their mountain in triumph, and I beam with adoration for my kids. They have grown up and are more capable now than they were a few short years ago. Little did we know something was waiting at the top of the rock pile that would shatter this moment into a million hysterical pieces.

The best thing to crap on your plans for happiness, fulfillment, and peace is just that: a massive pile of crap.

As they climb over the mound of rocks I hear a scream—one of the boys has tripped. I rush to make sure he isn't more seriously injured and discover not only is his knee covered in dog poop, but it is also all over his skin because of a hole in his jeans. For good measure, the poop is also curiously in the armpit of his jacket, which smears all over my hand as I haul him up to his feet.

I am usually so prepared when I leave the house with my kids. I carry everything I could ever need in my diaper bag, down to a miniature tape measure (because you never know when you might need to know the precise length of something less than three feet). But when you haul 80 pounds of anything farther than three feet, the idea of carrying *extra* baggage is ridiculous. I have nothing, not even a snot-soaked tissue in my pocket to help clean up the mess. I improvise and employ a few decomposing leaves from the mat of vegetation beside the trail. They promptly disintegrate as I mush the poop around my son's leg.

I wonder if crying is as contagious as yawning, because all three of my children erupt into tears in quick succession, and only one of them has a legitimate reason. My first son freaks out because…poop. My other son cries because the hike was cut short. Little Sister sobs because I picked her up and am not allowing her to walk by herself; her independence is crushed and she is likely scarred for life. In a futile attempt to control the situation, I yell in my "Sergeant Mom" voice for them all to calm down.

A little-known fact about poop: if it touches your extremities, it has a paralyzing effect. Poop has stolen my son's ability to walk, so I load my frantic boy into the wagon. We need a police escort, but there is only me to haul our troop out of nature and back to running water and wet wipes. My poop-covered son envisions a solo ride, but I need to move faster than a toddler. I can't carry her writhing little body *and* pull him along at the same time. She goes into the wagon, too; it only stands to reason. My son sits there wailing, his leaden arms and legs using every conceivable portion of space, no doubt in an effort to reduce the possibility of the poop spreading. He doesn't want her to sit with him, and it is clear she doesn't want to ride anyway, given the way her rigid frame refuses to bend into a seated position. As I push her down into the wagon, my son pushes her back up in protest. Somehow I load all three of them and head for home. When the trail gets too steep for me to pull all that weight, I plead for my poop-free son to get out and help push the wagon uphill. He cheerfully hops out, eager to get away from his brother, who reeks, and to escape the colossal fit his sister is throwing.

Our house has never looked so welcoming as we nearly skid to a stop at the door. I waste no time. Right there on the front porch in the middle of winter, I strip off everyone's clothes and consider whether or not I should burn them just in case. I put my daughter down for a nap, the boys in the shower, and sit on the couch to breathe another sigh of relief, glad to be back in the chaos I wanted to escape earlier in the day.

In life, you will be surprised by crap, and it will screw up your plans, and when it does, you just have to bear the stench until you can wash it off...or burn it.

# A REGULAR BAD DAY

*Robin Chapman*

ODAY WAS SUPPOSED TO BE DIFFERENT. I wanted quiet time, breakfast, and coffee before the kids woke so I could step into the morning with a calm, glad heart, and hope my children would follow my example. But a bad night with several kids coming to my side of the bed in the ungodly dark hours followed by a rough morning of bad behavior (not least of all my own) has set off a cascade of crap. You know how this goes: interrupted sleep is followed by early morning chaos that cruelly precludes coffee.

It's now 10:00 am. I've been parenting for hours. There have been wet beds and tantrums, defiance and messes. Breakfast happened with more than the average number of spills. I've discovered spilled oatmeal more than once with my bare feet. My highly sensitive nervous system is twitching, and I'm on the verge of shutting down. At least two of my four children are yelling at all times, and I can't seem to get us all reeled back in. My nerves are frayed and my responses less than gracious. Their behavior escalates along with mine until all five of us are yelling over each other and I hate everything.

I'm always surprised by how the little things throw me. I see my expectations dashed over and over in a million small ways, and I see how I come undone every. single. time.

It's not the big things that take me down. I can handle the urgent care trip when my 3-year-old, who lately has developed the notion that he's proficient with a knife, then mistakes his thumb for a carrot. I've managed long weeks keeping a newborn fed while juggling a household and recovering from birth.

The big things are catastrophic enough that it's pretty clear what needs my attention right this second. One morning, when my third (the aforementioned thumb-chopper) was just a couple weeks old, I sent my husband one of my standard inappropriately long texts: *"Hey. I just called the Birth Center. I figured out what my deal is—the sleeplessness and the irritability—it's postpartum anxiety. I didn't recognize it because I assumed I was immune after having no issues with the first two. I have an appointment at 12:15 because she needs to see me to prescribe. I'm going on Celexa. I don't have time for this crap to take me out like it is."* He replied with sensitivity that surprised me: *"I think it's courageous that you're getting the help you need."* In times of intense stress, I can dig deep and find what I need to walk forward—even when going forward means visiting a professional.

However, when life is just the normal chaos, I freeze. My movements and words become slow and deliberate, as if I'm trying to convince myself and an imaginary state trooper that I have not, in fact, been drinking. Internally, there's a storm of shouting and anger: *Why can't you just handle it? Why can't they just obey? Of course she spilled her milk. Of course she did. Why are these people so loud??? You're the one who decided four babies in a handful of years was a good idea!*

At 10:00 in the morning on a regular bad day, I'm hours from the partial respite of naptime for the little two and a LIFETIME away from the promised land of bedtime (or whatever point after bedtime they're all blessedly quiet). I'm struggling and learning (slowly) how to bounce back from this kind of mundane crisis.

The worst days end with me hiding in the bathroom, scrolling Facebook while the kids destroy everything.

On my best days, I remember the truth that I've been specifically chosen and equipped for this horde of noisy people (whom I love), and I remember the tools I've accrued. I don't have a special formula that reliably salvages our bad days, but I have slowly collected strategies that sometimes help when I'm desperate.


When my nerves are frayed, I get them outside or moving. My big two are old enough to be sent out on their own, so weather permitting, they burn energy outdoors with a decibel level meant to fill the Alaskan wilderness. I am thankful to avoid one thousand reminders to "use your INSIDE voice!" When the weather isn't cooperative, I devise games inside. Race up and down the hall. Jump on the trampoline. Do somersaults on the futon. Whatever, as long as it's silly and high-energy.

If the weather's bad and I can't manage the wild of an indoor obstacle course, I pull one kid out of the fray. No matter how many kids I have, one fewer always feels infinitely easier. Sometimes I can pull one aside (bonus if it's the instigator of the day) for a "special activity": something (real or fabricated) they can "help" with, or a coloring page I find online. This buys me the minutes and bandwidth I need to mitigate the chaos of the larger group and calm everything down.

If I'm feeling like an A+ mom, I give the kids a job. On mornings like this one, I usually don't have the bandwidth for that—my kids are in a phase where their enthusiasm is high, but their ability to actually help is quite low. All the same, shifting them toward productive work frequently helps their attitudes. Even though it requires a lot of effort for me to set them up with jobs they can (and want to) do, it's usually worthwhile for the change of atmosphere in our home. When they wash the dishes, it takes them about five times as long as it would take me. Yet with water everywhere, my fighting, whining children transform into proud, helpful ones. I'll take the puddles.

More frequently, I herd them toward read-aloud time. Sometimes I just start reading to see if anybody shows up. Sometimes it works. Sometimes it deteriorates into loud fights and complaints about the book choice. Just as often, they all get quiet for at least a few minutes.

Usually, one of these will give us enough of a reset that I can catch my breath, get a glass of water, maybe go to the bathroom. There's no magic here—the kids still need correction, and attitudes require work all around, but a tiny shift can drastically improve the trajectory of my day. If not, there's always Netflix.

This particular morning, I try a combination of things to keep my sanity intact. After ignoring them and trying really hard not to yell at them (completely failing at both),

I send some of them outside (but then they start fighting). I try to read out loud to them for ten minutes, until it is clear nobody is interested. There is coloring and discipline and a "highly recommended" living room cleanup session. (At least I play fun music while we do this? "I Like to Move It" is excellent for that.) None of these things magically solves all my problems—I live with four little kids; sometimes life is just like this—but we inch toward bedtime with only a *little* Netflix.

# WORSHIP AT THE KITCHEN SINK

*Emily Sue Allen*

I SHOW UP AT THE SINK TO AN INSURMOUNTABLE PILE OF dishes. Nothing is scraped. Nothing is sorted. My frustratingly miniscule counter space is overrun with remnants of our previous two meals—room-temp food, wadded up napkins between plates, stray silverware, and pans that need to be soaked. I pause and take a deep breath, aware that the only way to get out of this mess is to travel through it, bit by bit, plate by plate.

To my left, worship music plays softly through the Bluetooth speaker residing inside the cupboard of drinking glasses. I swing the cabinet door open so melodies can surround my weary soul as I swipe plates with a sponge and place them into the dishwasher. I'm hoping the cares I've brought to the kitchen will wash down the drain along with the bits of discarded food I scrape into the disposal.

I've never been great at staying ahead of the mayhem, and as we've added kids to our family, it has become increasingly difficult to keep a tidy kitchen (let alone a tidy house).

Most of the time I hobble along, performing whatever damage control is necessary to get through the day. Despite my best efforts, I constantly feel like our home is in disarray.

Like my kitchen, I am a mess inside—anxious, easily irritated by the squabbles of seven spirited children, weighed down by worries common to mothers everywhere.

Not a single thing I do in the course of a day leads to a satisfying end. I always have more toys to pick up, more laundry loads to flip, and more dishes to wash.

I turn up the volume loud enough to drown out the normal sounds of the kids, but not so loud I won't be able to hear if an emerging situation requires my attention. Words of hope fill my ears, and the music draws me into another world. I replace noise with noise, but the worshipful words are a solace and an invitation to quiet my heart before God while my hands do the work they know well. I am transported to a place where I am both physically present in an ordinary kitchen task and attentive to a deeper exchange between His spirit and mine.

When I show up at my kitchen sink, God shows up too.

We've always had one of those dishwashers that requires us to thoroughly pre-wash the dishes before adding them to the racks. This past summer, the dishwasher broke and was out of commission for several weeks, prompting a change in my dishwashing routine.

Everything had to be thoroughly washed and dried by hand. The job required even more of my time than usual. I gave myself to carefully washing every dish with a slow swath of suds, a thorough rinse, and delicate dry with a towel before putting it away to be used the next time.

As I did so, it occurred to me that this is how God

cleanses me: personally, gently, completely. I know more acutely than anyone how much I need His cleansing and His grace—much more often than my kitchen needs attention.

When I plunge my hands into soapy water to wipe dishes clean, I pray. I offer God my anxious thoughts and the worries that too easily rule me. I surrender my sense of entitlement to a day that doesn't challenge my patience. I ask for help and a willing heart that will not resist the constant care and leadership my children require.

Standing at the sink, I do some of my most important business of the day. Here, God teaches me about faithfulness and cultivates the heart of a servant within me.

Servants cannot do what they please. They must faithfully do what is required of them, or they are not truly serving. I experience this tension every day, recognizing I can embrace the responsibilities before me, or I can fight against the invitation to serve my family in the humble ways God asks.

When I resist the tasks that need to be done in the kitchen or elsewhere in my home, I veer off in the direction of self-pity and discouragement, allowing a complaining attitude to sneak into my heart in the midst of my weariness. But when I apply myself to stewarding my home and family, doing ordinary work with faithfulness, I yield to the process of God strengthening my character. This is where my vision for attentive, intentional motherhood is sharpened. This is where I discover hidden treasures of humility.

My kitchen sink is an unlikely sacred space, but it has certainly become sacred to me.

My heart is changed—transformed from heavy, broken,

run-down, and discouraged to something lighter, something different. I may arrive at the sink reluctantly, but as I scrub away bits of food from breakfast and pause within my heart to hear God's voice, I breathe in grace, renewal, and perspective about who I am, what I'm doing, and why I'm doing it.

When I became a mother, I didn't know I would be taking on the role of a full-time servant. Motherhood is as much about building my character as it is about caring for children. God has called me to faithfulness in the daily work of tending a family, and these humble household tasks are not beneath me.

Dishes must be done.

In order to fuel me through the hard days of motherhood, I draw strength and inspiration from the example of Jesus as a servant.

During an evening meal with His disciples, Jesus poured water into a basin and began to wash their feet. At first, they resisted, but He gently pressed on to model the practice of humility. He encouraged the disciples to follow His example by serving one another in ordinary ways.

Doing what is needed at the kitchen sink—or any other part of the home—is the worship of a humble servant. The daily, necessary tasks of caring for a family are the building blocks of motherhood. This is faithfulness. This is love. This is significant, holy work.

When I flip the water off and dry my hands, I know I'll be back in a few hours' time. But I also know the unending nature of this cycle is grace—worshipful repetition at the kitchen sink as I cultivate the heart I desire to bring to motherhood: a heart to serve.

# HIS ONLY MOM

*Bethany McMillon*

FROM THE WOODEN WRAP-AROUND PORCH, I peek through the front-door window. I spot him easily. His bald head, chubby legs, and toothless grin draw my eye. He's bouncing in her lap; she's holding his hands. They're smiling and talking back and forth. My heart soars at this sight just before I open the door. I know once I do, his smiles will be for me. He will reach for me, his little fists will curl up into my hair, and he'll snuggle into my chest, ready to go home. Since I've gone back to work, most days are like this.

When I first calculated my son's due date, I was thrilled. An April birth date meant I'd take maternity leave as school ended *and* receive the bonus gift of summer break to stay home with him a little longer. Then I'd return to my teaching job in the fall. The extra weeks with him felt like the promise of a gift. To prepare for his daycare experience, I did all the proactive-mom things. I researched the ratings of local daycares, talked endlessly with other mom friends to ask for their personal recommendations, and compiled an exhaustive list of questions to ask potential caregivers. My husband and I weighed the options of in-home daycare or a daycare center. I visited several potential options and sobbed after visiting one that simply wouldn't work for our family. (The crying may have been more over the knowledge my return to work was best for our family.) Coupled with the demands of pregnancy, the whole process was emotional and overwhelming.

As July came to a close, I turned the calendar on the fridge to August—the month when he would begin daycare and I would go back to work. It felt like just yesterday we'd brought him home. It had taken both parents to manage the first diaper change and the first few feedings. That first night, we both lay sideways on the bed, peered into the bassinet and marveled at his existence—and that he was sleeping! Little did we know that night would be the only time for months he would sleep so many hours in a row. Now, we have a routine for almost everything—nighttime feedings, bottle making, diaper changing, and even the songs I sing to him while I make dinner. The time has gone more quickly than I could have thought possible. His first day would be a half-day, to ease us both into our new schedule and allow me to work at school before students arrived in a few days. After months of marking every milestone and moment on this calendar, I dutifully—and with trepidation—marked his first day too.

I arrived that first morning fully prepared with everything all the lists told me to bring. Over one shoulder, I slung a diaper bag full of carefully labeled daily essentials: pre-made bottles in an insulated cooler, a small, pale blue bowl of nearly liquid cereal mixed with just a smidge of blended fruit, a few changes of clothes, and a handful of burp cloths. Looped over the other arm, I carried my baby boy—wide-eyed and securely nestled in his car seat—and used my hip to balance a carton of diapers and sensitive-skin wipes. I had cross-checked the daycare's list of suggested supplies with internet recommendations, just to make sure the professional caregivers did actually know what they were talking about. And I brought extras…so many extras.

Loaded down with enough supplies for quadruplets, I was already sweating in the early morning Texas heat before I reached the gate of the white picket fence.

Eva, the daycare center director, greeted me with a smile and proposed a sweet plan for distracting my son while I left. Her kindness drew him out of my arms and straight into hers. Though her instructions sounded simple enough, "Kiss him goodbye and don't linger these first few times. We'll take good care of him," they were hard to follow. *What if she doesn't know the exact temperature he likes his bottle? What if she doesn't know the difference in his hungry, tired, and hurt cries? What if they feed him the wrong child's formula, leaving us to struggle with tummy troubles for days?*

Despite my worries, I followed her suggestions. Taking his sweet face in my hands, I kissed both his pink cheeks and his forehead, pausing just a second to soak in his scent and the smoothness of his skin, and I returned to my car feeling victorious. I'd done it! He was there safely and *look at me!* I wasn't even crying! My brain switched gears to teacher mode. My list of things to get done at school was long, since I hadn't stepped foot in the building since April. Plus, I wanted to take a few minutes to reward myself with a stop for my favorite coffee.

The four hours I planned to be gone flew by. I pulled into a parking space next to the white picket fence with satisfaction. I'd accomplished a major feat as a working mom—day one at daycare.

With pep in my step, I walked up the whitewashed wood-plank sidewalk. My boy sat snuggled into Eva's lap reading a book. His eyes, fully focused on the colors of the animals being identified in Spanish, didn't look up until I called out, "Hey, bubba!" His arms flailed and flapped and he reached for me to pick him up. I hugged him and smothered him in kisses. Eva recounted the details of his day and slipped the daily report into his diaper bag. I thanked her, walked back out to the car, and tucked him into his car seat.

Then a thought hit me like a hammer. *He didn't even seem to miss me! He didn't cry this morning when I dropped him off. He was perfectly comfortable in her lap when I picked him up. What if he doesn't love me as much because I'm choosing to go back to work?*

I caught his reflection in the rearview mirror contentedly dozing as we drove home. My mind swirled with insecurity. At home, he transferred beautifully from car seat to crib for an afternoon nap. I sank down onto the couch. The phone rang and I jumped, startled out of thought.

"Hello?" I whispered, as if my attempt at quiet would offset the screaming of the phone ringing.

"Hey, sweetie, how did today go?" My mom's soothing voice opened the floodgate of emotions as I explained the tornado of thoughts in my mind. She listened and understood.

Finally, as my words turned from a flood to a trickle, she said, "Bethy-girl, you are his *Mama*. He may love every minute of his time there—just as he does here at my house.

But no one can replace you. You are his only *Mom*."

My spirit quieted. I am his mom.


Day by day, drop-off became easier. Eventually, we settled into a routine in which my husband drops him off each day. When I pick him up each afternoon, I visit with Eva and the other women who have become friends. My little guy loves Eva deeply. Before he could crawl, he'd roll himself across the floor to wherever she was. She'd laugh and pull him up to snuggle him close. My heart chooses to believe he is her favorite too.

We're seven months after that first hard day now. As I pause to peek through the window, watching his caregivers coo and play and meet his needs, I have peace and a grateful heart for all those who love him well—and I'm already looking forward to next summer's extra time with my little guy. The spring sun and warm breeze remind me our summer is just 11 weeks away, and Spring Break starts right now.

# HUG ARMS

*Melissa Hogarty*

S HE IS JUMPING WILDLY UP AND DOWN, clutching the edge of the kitchen table, screaming, "I. Need. A. HUG!"

I am standing 18 inches away from her with my arms outstretched, trying to find an opening to give her what she claims to want.

It's a trick, of course. She doesn't want a hug. She wants to scream. But I believe in hugs, so I offer anyway. If I could change this morning with a hug, I would. A hug is an easy gift to give.

She races away, still hollering. Her feet pound like she is on a pogo stick as she springs to throw herself against an armchair so she can yell about hugging me from farther away.

Neither of us is even sure why she's upset. Because she didn't want to get dressed? Because she's hungry? Because she's 3?

She begins to play the piano. Her hug demands be-

85

come almost melodic. "I WAAAANT a HUUUUUG!" she hollers as she bangs on the keys.

I don't pursue her. But my arms still want to give her that hug.

After she finally gives up and eats her breakfast, she wants to color. She squeezes her knees together and bounces a little (a telltale sign she needs to go potty), begging for coloring paper while I rinse dirty dishes. I take her into the bathroom.

"But I don't need to go!"

"We try when we're dry," I remind her in a singsong voice, trying to keep my own spirits high. This morning feels like yet another in a long line of emotionally weary mornings. In the war of attrition she is waging against me, my attitude is usually the first casualty. I wonder if she knows how long I hold out. I wonder if she can see how hard I fight to do it right for her. Or does she only count the times I lose the battle?

"Please! Please! PleeeeeAAAAASSE!" she whines from the potty. "Help! Mommy, help!"

I confess I am not quite sure how to help. If I could pee for her, potty training would be a lot easier.

She starts whimpering—she hates the toilet and begs to get off the second she sits down—and calls my name as pitifully as she can manage in a little, crackly voice. "AH ah. AH ah. Moooommy."

"How can I help you?"

"I need help!" she insists. I repeat my question, rubbing her knee and looking into her eyes so she knows I am serious. I will help her if I can. I want this to work. I want her to be confident and successful—on the potty and everywhere else.

"I just want you to do NOTHING."

Okay…I can do that. I sit on the stool by the sink, calmly picking at my fingernails while I wait for her to do her business.

"No, Mom, I just want you to do NOTHING!" she yells at me again. I can feel my inner order starting to slide.

"I am *not* doing anything," I respond, a little impatiently. After all, not doing anything is pretty hard when you're a mom. Usually, every single fold of my mental space is occupied with the next steps I need to take, even as my hands are busy with the previous ones. I am stacking dishes on the drying rack and then planning to rip out that coloring page she wants, and afterward I will check the sheets in the dryer, and when I bring the sheets upstairs, I must not forget to bring a box of tissues back down, and oh! I should also bring the battery box back to the closet when I go up, and on and on and on.

Doing nothing requires focus.

But my nothing is not good enough for her. I banish myself from the bathroom, because I am not sure of another way to fulfill her request to help by doing nothing. And, let's be honest, because I am starting to feel a little henpecked. By a 3-year-old.

Of course, the moment I walk out, she is whining my name again. My name has become slime. It stretches out of her mouth and dribbles stickily to coat my ears. I would scrub that sound away if I could. *Mommyyyy. Mooommmmmmyyyy.*

"Mommy, I need heeeeeelp."

*Guess what, little girl? Mommy needs a minute to herself.*

She continues to call me. I close my eyes and imagine myself being calm. And then I snap them open and scream

STRONG, BRAVE & BEAUTIFUL

her name and shout as loud as I can that she must stop shouting at me.

"But I neeeeeed a huuuuuuug!" she warbles.

I pull her off the potty. "I don't know how to give you what you want!" I cry desperately. "You asked for a hug and then ran away! You told me to do nothing, so I left! Don't tell me to leave if you want me here! How can I do what you want when you tell me the opposite?!"

As I hear my voice climbing in pitch and beginning to sound a bit hysterical, I also listen to my words. A small force inside my brain pushes back.

Wait a minute. My job isn't to give her everything she wants. Does she know this?

She doesn't have any idea what my job is. And I start to realize that I don't quite know how to define it, either. If I list off all the tasks I regularly perform, I sound quite important. Chef, Maid, Governess, Nurse. Chauffeur, Accountant, Manager. Personal Trainer, Event Planner, Life Coach, Spiritual Director. Entertainer. Human.

I think about telling her my job is to keep her alive. It sounds both melodramatic and insufficient to my ears.

But what *is* my job?

Being her mom is so much more than I can put into words.

I am turning a tiny blank slate into a fully formed person. I am helping her learn how to interpret the world and how to be kind and how to use the right word to say what she means. I teach her how the letters of the alphabet sound and how to follow through on a task and, yes, how to use her body. I am only partway through, and I'm not sure how well I am doing. Motherhood is both harder and more magical than I expected.

I am learning too. *She* is turning *me* into a fully formed person. I am learning that I cannot control everything. I am learning that I, too, have big emotions. I am learning to put down the other thing I want to do and look my children in the eyes and not regret this change of pace.

That's really the kicker, the very hardest lesson about humility and selflessness in this stage of motherhood. To not resent the children who want my attention. They want my whole heart, and they want it now.

I am their mother. It is my job to show them love, no matter which buttons they press. I must train them when they don't know better, and train them when they test boundaries, and train them when they do it wrong on purpose, with the same heart as the very first time I began the lesson. It isn't glamorous. It's hard to define. But my job is really just…to be present.

So, little daughter, my arms are still open. You can scream at me or run away, but I will still love you. I will sit with you when you need me, even when it is inconvenient. I will help you when I can, even though sometimes that help will be hard for both of us.

My hug arms are waiting when you are ready.

# COMING OUT OF HIS SHELL

*Jacelya Jones*

THERE'S A SMELL IN MY SON'S ROOM LIKE THE WINDOWS need to be cranked open wide for a day and night of fresh air. It looks "clean" in a way that makes me suspicious—the way the comforter's hanging and the bed skirt is bulging. The bathroom and closet doors are closed, I note. *That can't be good.*

What seemed tidy at first glance begins to reveal itself as I move farther into the room: underwear, t-shirts, footie pajamas, a pile of sheets peeking out from under the blue and white whales swimming on his beanbag. I stop and stare, looking for clues about the extent of the mess without opening the doors, my lips pressing into a line that draws wrinkles at the corners of my mouth. They match the ones at my eyes. My "tell" is firing, revealing the depth of my anxiety—I'm smoothing the hair at the nape of my neck, thoughtfully playing piano back there with my fingers. I open my mouth to mutter something, inhale, then exhale a sigh.

On my way out, I stop to look at Flash the Tortoise slowly scratching across its grainy bedding toward its food plate. From there, the creature tries to gain enough height to liberate itself. I always think it's looking at me, begging for its freedom or begging for someone to see it and tend to its lonely heart. Pellet poop dotted in that grainy bedding is evidence of neglect.

My son says he loves the tortoise, but it's hard to believe with the way he forgets to pick up after it and has to be reminded to give it a nice handful of lettuce every day.

Frustration rises up and takes hold of my voice, surprising me. I shout, making the pragmatic blocks of his name stand up in prominent syllables. My hands go to my hips as I shift gears from Uncertain Investigator of the Boy Habitat straight to Judge. I prepare to make a pronouncement against the lawbreaker.

"Yes, Mama?" he asks from the doorway, not winded from his run up the stairs. His big eyes are wide, filled with hope that this encounter will go well. Those eyes drown any real fire in my soul.

With my face scrunched up like the light is too bright for my eyes, I say, "You forgot to feed Flash."

His face drops, and his dejectedness mixes ashes into the embers of my temper.

*How can we break this cycle?* I wonder. *Why does your candle go out so easily? If I breathe wrong, you go dim.*

"I'm sorry," he says before I can finish speaking. Apologies run in his blood these days.

"You don't have to be sorry," I say, like I always do, but the words have lost their meaning through overuse. I try something different: "What can we—*you* do to remind yourself of all the things you need to do every day?" I keep saying "we," before I realize it and correct myself. It's his work to do, not mine. "Do you think if we—*you* write a note to yourself and hang it up where you see it in the morning, we—*you* can remember to brush your teeth and clean your room and feed your animal?"

He's not making eye contact anymore. He shrugs and mumbles something. He looks totally defeated. I feel defeated.

*You can stop, Mama,* I hear in his sorries. *I know I'm bad*—as if failure is who and what he is.

Later, as we're clearing up homeschool papers, textbooks, and pencils, Baby Sister knocks over his cup of water, which should not have been on the kitchen table amid schoolwork.

"Honey, get a towel from the laundry room. Don't you see the water coming toward your workbook?"

"I'm sorry!" he snaps with barely leashed emotion in his eyes and voice.

"Listen, I'm trying to help, but I don't always know how to talk to you," I say. "You're a young man, and I have to be your mama in a different way."

"I don't think I'm a man. I'm always doing bad things," he says.

I resist the urge to roll my eyes. "Honey, we all do the wrong thing sometimes," I say instead. "I'm your mama. It's my job to help you look at a situation and make good choices. I want you to stop fighting with me," I say, shadow-boxing with the moves Billy Blanks and Tae Bo taught me. "I don't want you to talk back or cry—"

"I'm not," he interrupts. I take a deep breath to keep myself from raising my voice.

"I said that after I said two *other* things. Did you hear

me say I don't want you to fight with me or to talk back?"

"I'm sorry," he says with the Face Drop. This time, my heart doesn't drop with him. I'm tracking this *Groundhog Day* scene better than I ever have. "I didn't mean to say that," my son blurts before I can respond.

"I'm not trying to make you feel bad." I wonder if his sadness is on me or if the hurt was already waiting under the surface, expecting to break free. "Let me help you organize your brain to think about problems. Pick up the things that might get destroyed. Then get the water."

It is a new approach for me: speaking into responses, trying to get his thoughts back on track where they've been derailed by emotion. I watch my son as he listens to my calm words. His face transforms from a fretful boy into that of a collected young man before my eyes.

Inadequacy often stalks me as I make my way along this new, tricky rite of passage. Past events have triggered me into babying him: while he was playing at their house, the kids who lived there threw shoes and buckets of water at him. He's been called "dummy" by classmates, not picked by peers to join their group for class projects, given the inadequate option of working alone at a table in the back of the room.

I wonder if all these moments have birthed the voices in his head, if the trauma of his experiences makes the light in his eyes dim with guilt or shame. God is helping me sort out the root causes of the "sorries" that come from my son so often. I'm learning to help my son reshape input into thoughts and responses that make him more resilient and less sorry. Resilience is learning from what crushes us, allowing our broken bones to be reset into a scaffold supporting humility instead of complacency, and allowing what spills out of our hearts to ferment into compassion.

As my son comes out of his shell toward the light of adulthood, the heavy lifting is shifting to him—with me as a bystander in many ways.

My son follows me outside to help me gather strawberries for our lunch. Everything about the scene—the sun, the fruit, and his happiness—compels me to grab my Nikon. This doesn't surprise him at all. He's patient with me as I ask him to move closer, left, and right. Suddenly, as I'm looking through the lens, I see his handsome face, the little boy and the young man inseparable in my eyes. I also see the future, when a tall, handsome, still-patient man will no longer need me to train him and take care of him. We are already starting to move in that direction.

My current job title is "empath." I have to hear him, be present, and make myself available without interpreting and fixing it all for him. I have to take a step back, so he can begin to believe he can take control of his life and choices. Otherwise, I will constrain his growth like a seedling too big for its terrarium.

I can't do everything for him, like how he takes care of his tortoise. Instead, I'm transitioning into a new season, guiding him over to the other side of boyhood. Now I encourage him to stand strong in godly character—responsibility, internal motivation, and strength. Sometimes, instead of wiping his tears, I tell him not to cry; instead of feeding and cleaning up after him, I must give him the space to practice what he has learned.

I am surprised at how much things have changed in just a few years. My son is coming out of his shell; he is a young man. What felt like creeping along at the tortoise's pace really happened in a flash.

# BARF DAYS

*Robin Chapman*

As I ROCK MY TODDLER BEFORE BED, the thought comes from nowhere. *You know, we haven't had a stomach bug in a while...*

On its heels: *CRAP. That's always what I think right before we get one.*

Like clockwork, the barfing begins the next morning (well, middle of the night). I almost laugh at my magical fortune-telling superpowers, but I can barely manage to run back and forth between the preschooler in the tub and the soiled bedding. *Good Lord, the bedding. What did she eat?!? I don't remember having anything like that for dinner. And it's all down the walls and the sides of the mattress and...*

Sanitize cycle. We just, for the first time in 15 years of marriage, got a brand-new washer and dryer, and it has an "oxi-sanitize" cycle to which I add an oxygenating laundry-boosting powder and some puke-laden towels. It runs for two and a half hours and magically kills whatever caused my kid to expel the contents of her stomach. I marvel at the timing, thankful the bug waited until the week *after* the new washer and dryer were installed.

The next morning finds me still cleaning. My sorta-smart watch says I slept for three hours, divided among five different stretches. I pass out the square plastic bowls we routinely use for catching puke (and also for leftovers). The count is now three kids down, Daddy in bed dying—I don't begrudge him this because I'm a bigger nausea/vomiting weenie than he is—one kid still apparently healthy, and me.

I feel mildly queasy. I don't know if it's because I've been thinking about vomit all day (and have cleaned it out of my bra once already) or because I'm the next victim. Honestly, I'm not sure which I prefer. I don't want to be down and still have to clean all this up, but I also hate the waiting. As I mentioned, I'm the biggest wuss about nausea—I spend any and all periods of sickness wondering if I'm going to die, hoping the answer is *yes*, and *soon*. If I'm gonna get this bug, I might as well have it over with.

As I wait for the answer to the "Am I sick or not?" question, I flit like a large, sleep-deprived hummingbird between the three sick children while also trying to keep the one healthy kid out of mischief. Everyone is in jammies, Netflix is on (a standard sick-day provision), and applesauce cups are what's for breakfast.

In a lull between stomach projections, I look at my kids lying on the floor in various states of malaise, and I feel… settled. Happy? *That's weird.*

If there's a lower form of service than stomach-bug mothering, I'm not sure what it is. But while I would never say I look forward to them, I've found the barf days are, in some ways, my best days.

On these days, I'm fully engaged in caring for the physical needs of my children; no other option is available. I rely on the grace of God to pull me through what's bound to be a difficult day—again, I am low on alternatives. This is not the kind of day I can handle on my own with barely a nap's worth of broken sleep. Because of those two realities—full presence and reliance on grace—I find myself spontaneously, compulsively, perpetually grateful for every. little. thing. The sanitize cycle on my brand-new washer. Exactly as many towels as I need. (I use them as drop cloths for the kids too small to reliably hit a container, and the very last one is fouled moments after the new dryer sings the "cycle finished" song.) My friend swings by to deliver coffee (my first of the day!) even though we canceled our get-together so she wouldn't be exposed to the nastiness. My normally active kids are cuddly. I have water that is clean, running, and *hot*, so I can wash off these disgusting children.

The root of the word "humble" is Latin: *humus*. Ground. These are humble days. When I'm low to the ground and my pride is out of the way, I find myself with only one direction to look: upward. And when I'm looking up, I see gifts as He gives them.

The bug turns out to be mercifully short, which is always my hope. By the afternoon, they are keeping down liquids; they eat some applesauce and toast right around the time I get sick for real. My husband recovers about the same time the kids do, so I tag out and whimper in our bed for several hours. That one kid never gets it. I don't know why, but I'm thankful.

# PART III

# DIGGING UP THE WEEDS

*Emily Sue Allen*

M Y OLDEST SONS ARE 19 MONTHS APART. They are spaced closer than any other pair of siblings in the family, and at 8 and 9 years old, their relationship is hot and cold—an adventure of hills and valleys in the same day and sometimes the same hour. One moment, they're best pals; the next, they're slugging each other in the shoulder and wrestling for the same chair at the table, each claiming it was "their spot."

As their mother, it warms my heart when they play joyfully together. Nothing like a buddy to crash your cars with. However, when they start whining, bickering, and picking mercilessly at each other, I feel anger swell within me.

The squabbles are always petty. The stakes, as of yet, have been low, but the distress brought on by their fighting scores high.

"HEY!" my older son shouts emphatically from his wobbly bike. Number two brother has accidentally (or perhaps not) clipped his rear tire while riding close behind.

Number one brother changes position to ride directly behind him, so he might exact stealthy revenge at an unexpected time. It's a constant cat and mouse game, only they switch roles often.

The flashpoint is low, and the threshold for eruptions of anger is easily crossed.

Often, my older son baits the younger. He'll hold something hidden in his palm and pretend to possess something belonging to his brother, cooly taunting him about what it might be.

"SHOW ME WHAT YOU HAVE," the younger will sputter, chasing the hidden hand while the older one gets a smug look on his face and pulls away.

"SHOW. ME. WHAT. YOU. HAAAAVE!"

I cringe and wish I could duck into a quiet room away from the fighting.

Minutes later, the instigator of the former conflict (the older of the two) is crying to me about his paper airplane, which he claims his younger brother stepped on. On *purpose.*

"Well, son, do you remember when, just a few minutes ago, you were being unkind to him and pretending to have something that belongs to him hidden in your hand?"

"I didn't do *anything,*" he says in a whiney voice, half rolling his eyes.

"Do you think maybe you contributed to this conflict?" I suggest again.

"It's not my fault, Mom. He stepped on *my* airplane and now it's *RUINED. UUUGGHH!*" His overexaggerated sigh-turned-growl is more than I can take.

Brother Two has been at the table, drawing a comic strip and minding his own business. He gets up to use the bathroom, and Brother One sees an opportunity to sit in *the* chair where the art supplies are set up. Mind you, there are seven other available seats at the table, but none of those chairs comes with a side of little-brother protest.

I close my eyes, draw in a slow breath, and long for an easy way out of this moment because I'm not sure I have it in me to be patient or calm. *Help me, Jesus.*

Brother One often complains about Brother Two without taking any responsibility for his own actions. According to him, it's always someone else's fault. *Of course it is.*

When Brother Two screeches upon return, I find myself teetering at the edge of my patience.

The whole summer has been challenging, and I'm desperate for a change or even a brief reprieve from the constant bickering. I have employed every trick I can think of to stave off the fighting, without success. I'm worn down to the point of staring blankly while my sons each raise their present complaints.

Behind my irritated expression, I stew a furious mess of emotions that I keep to myself for the moment.

I have to do something to help us change course, but I don't know what. I feel like I've tried everything—time-outs, extra (positive) attention, teamwork training, yelling, incentives, loss of privileges, lines of copywork, early bed-time—nothing has worked. My eyes dart around the house in search of some way to ensure a small reprieve from the bickering. I look at my older son.

"Work gloves. Weeds. Outside."

I snap up the gloves with determination, hoping a little time outside in the yard will help my older son start in a new direction. I have to separate them. I have to try *something*. I can't continue this daily pattern of discord. Fortunately, my husband is home, and I leave the other kids with him.

We arrive at the dandelion haven outside our front door. An eager crew of children has spread the dandelion seeds across the lawn on many wish-blowing occasions, and those seeds have now sprouted up. Paul's words from Galatians 6:8 spring to mind: "For the one who sows to his own flesh will from the flesh reap corruption, but the one who sows to the Spirit will from the Spirit reap eternal life." As we have sown, so we are reaping. *Indeed.* The feathery, bright yellow blooms brush against my legs, and even though I've passed by this stretch of our property dozens of times this week, I see for the first time just how many dandelions have grown. It's been a month since the last mow, and these weeds have vigorously taken over the yard.

Who knew that if you let weeds grow where they land, they multiply at an alarming rate?

We find a dense patch and sit down. At first, I think I'm going to watch him do the task. I settle into a collapsible chair with a book and watch while he struggles to get one dandelion pulled up from the grass. I'm still wound up from weeks of his challenging behavior, and what I really want is an instant change without any fuss. Within a few minutes, I realize my son needs me to set my annoyance aside and yank out the weeds alongside him. Thus far, he's broken off every stem at the base, and hasn't gotten the roots of a single weed.

I realize he needs my instruction and my example. He needs my encouragement and my help to stay focused. After a few fruitless yanks of my own, our next door neighbor breaks from her mid-afternoon run to offer us a brilliant tool from her gardening shed, designed to efficiently dig out dandelions. As we sort out the mess of this yard, I realize our hearts—his *and* mine—are both full of things that need to be dealt with. We are *both* in need of God's transformative work in us.

He is bright, interesting, and delightful. He is also selfish, prideful, and occasionally mean-spirited. Me? I'm a good mom: attentive, caring, and committed. I am also irritable, short-tempered, and raise my voice more than I'd like to. All that to say, we both have our flaws. We each have to account for our own actions and choose a different route if we hope to cultivate strong relationships.

Children are individuals, and the fabric of their personhood deserves respect and care. I recognize I influence who my children will become. I can't afford to ignore the ways they require my love and leadership, even when it is inconvenient or frustrating. They need me to be in the dirt with them, present and patient through the ups and downs. If I am too distant or distracted, I can't help them realize their potential. If I set too high a standard and I'm not there to help them reach it, they will lose heart and quit trying.

This is my resolve: I will be close. I will be present and engaged. I will instruct, encourage, and lead by example, with dirt under my fingernails and grass stains on my jeans if that's what it takes. This is the work of an intentional mama—digging up the weeds.

# IT IS WELL

*Mary Kate Brown*

M Y YOUNGEST DAUGHTER CLIMBS ALL OVER ME WITH
an insatiable curiosity as I struggle to keep her
little baby hands away from IV lines. My oldest daughter
stares at me, wearing a hesitant expression. She worries she
might hurt me if she comes any closer. Meanwhile, my
middle daughter obliviously scans my side table for snacks.

The visit does not last long enough to ease the ache my
heart feels after being separated from them for so many
days. At the same time, their energetic presence in my tiny
hospital room completely exhausts me. I let out a sigh of
relief, guilt, and sadness as they follow my husband and
mother-in-law out of my room—relief they are gone, guilt
because I feel relieved, and sadness because they are no
longer with me.

Alone and feeling utterly defeated, I contemplate how
Crohn's disease has stolen my peace of mind and my health,
and how this current hospital stay is robbing me of time

with my kids. I am not prepared for the two months that will follow this stay—more hospital admissions, surgeries, and appointments with a number of specialists.

During my very first hospital stay three years ago (before I was diagnosed), I was terrified I might've had appendicitis. I felt certain an appendectomy would be the worst thing that could happen to me at that time. *Little did I know.*

My appendix, though healthy, would end up being collateral damage in the procedures I'd eventually need as a result of complications from my illness. Crohn's disease demanded more from me physically, mentally, and spiritually than I could have ever imagined. Ultimately, I'd have three surgical procedures performed to remove the damage done to my body, *by* my body, before I turned 30 years old.

Over the course of these two months in and out of hospitals, I underwent the first two of three total surgeries I needed that spring. The first surgery failed, and the second kept my condition stable until I was able to see a different surgeon at a university hospital where I would have the third surgery performed. During this in-between time, I had to wear a surgical drain semi-permanently fixed in the right side of my belly above my hip and held in place by thick black stitches. The drain was large and unsightly. It helped keep the infection at bay until I could have the surgery that would fix me, but it was utterly mortifying. It was also quite painful. I struggled to find clothing that would hide the drain and, because of my embarrassment, we stayed cooped up in our house.

My treatment became so physically demanding that I

was forced to stop breastfeeding earlier than I would have liked. I was supposed to be homeschooling my other two daughters, but my recoveries were far from quick, and we all became a little too familiar with Netflix. I vacillated between feeling strong enough to make it through a day and being so sick I could do little more than peel bananas for my kids while lying in bed. The rhythms of our life abruptly shifted from stable to unpredictable.

Several weeks went on like this, and I grew increasingly frustrated. This disease had dictated how I lived my life and how I mothered my children. Typically, we'd visit the park or library, but most days I felt too embarrassed to go out in public—even when I felt well enough to leave home. Eventually, I'd had enough of our forced isolation: hiding at home with shame, keeping company with fear, and struggling alone with both physical and emotional pain.

The first Sunday back in church after a number of missed weeks, I released everything: my attempt to control the situation, my vanity and embarrassment, my disappointment and anger and self-berating. I stood in the first row of the dimly lit sanctuary during worship with a giant, unconcealable surgical drain hanging from my right hip. Voices, piano, and bass drowned out the heavy sobs swelling from deep within my chest. Hot tears streamed down my cheeks, and with them poured the brokenness I felt physically and emotionally. "God, I don't know how to carry this burden. I've tried and failed. You can have it all—not just the struggle, but any good part of me too." My voice strained from sobbing, I barely managed to sing along with the music: "It is well."

*It is well. Even with me.*

Though nothing had changed inside my body, some-

,hing shifted in my spirit. The words "It is well" became a prophetic declaration over my body and mind that determined how this situation would ultimately turn out for me: well.

I was given new grace to move forward that morning. I stopped hiding. I stopped keeping my health a secret. I stopped shutting myself and my girls inside in order to save face. I released my control over a situation where I had none to begin with. From that morning on, I refused to let my unfavorable circumstance get in the way of my life and my motherhood if I could help it.

We spent the following four weeks before the big surgery at the library, going to parks, running errands, and visiting with friends. My kids and I even made new friends while out and about, despite my unsightly-but-necessary medical accessory. I allowed people to visit me. I received meals and prayers. I asked for help with babysitting. It was when I acknowledged I couldn't hold it all together that things suddenly came together. In a work of grace, this challenging situation worked out for our good right in the middle of the mess. I started experiencing wellness before my physical body was made well again.

I still find myself living the lessons I learned during this difficult season that, at the time, seemed so fruitless. I once believed resilience was only found in persisting against unfavorable circumstances. I've been humbled to learn it also looks like relinquishing false refuges of control and appearances. Sometimes resilience looks like letting go and not holding it all together. In our surrender we're better able to take hold of strength from outside of us that sustains through turmoil. Resilience is standing to declare all will be well in the midst of life's storms.

# EVEREST

*Lynne Patti*

T HE PAIN IS UNBEARABLE. As I sit with my Boppy and my baby on the couch, my newborn daughter and I attempt to achieve a good suck-swallow pattern for what seems like the 3,948th time today. I hold my breath as I try to get her latched on the right side—one last try this morning—the pain radiating through my whole body.

*This isn't working.*

We've been sitting here for nearly an hour, and I have to believe she's gotten *some* nutrition, but she is clearly not satisfied. I gently put her down in the baby swing and begin my walk of shame to the kitchen, where I make a bottle of formula to top her off. My hike to the kitchen stalls as I notice an Everest-sized pile of clean laundry, begging to be folded. I also pass by forgotten mail (read: bills) on the table, spilled cat food on the floor (probably kicked over by accident in a sleepy haze), smelly rags piling up on the kitchen counter, and, of course, a sink full of dirty dishes. I feel a weight in the center of my chest. Every step is heavy and laborious as the mountain of tasks starts to suffocate me. The jingly tune of the washing machine reminds me to get the wash into the dryer ASAP because otherwise, I'll forget to flip it and the clothes will get stinky (like the last time). I'm struggling to keep up.

I feel my breath begin to shorten and catch. Anxiety mixes with panic and rises up through my throat, bringing tears as I brace myself against the kitchen counter.

*There's just so much to do. My baby isn't nursing well. I don't know how to get up this mountain. I am not cut out for any of this.*

In the other room, my baby mirrors my crying. Sobs wrack my body so violently, I can't even breathe.


My first step out of overwhelm was a call to a lactation consultant. She offered me calm, steady words of wisdom to help me move forward.

Among other bits of helpful advice, she said, "New mamas need as much care as their babies. Make sure you take a breath here and there. Take a break."

*How am I supposed to care for myself right now? I can't even breathe, let alone...what? Take a bubble bath or paint my toes?*

In the six weeks since my baby girl had arrived, I was solely focused on her needs—attempting to get some sort of milk into her each day, tending her at every hour of the night, changing her, and trying desperately to keep from suffocating under my own overwhelm. I also subconsciously believed my husband "shouldn't have to" do anything baby-related, but rather focus on his career. The beginning of this motherhood climb was proving extremely difficult.

*How do I take a breath? Take a break?*

One afternoon, after two and a half months of feeling around in the dark for some kind of relief from the constant grind of round-the-clock care, I finally took a breath.

"We really need some groceries," I told my husband as I placed six pre-made formula bottles in the fridge.

Nursing had slowly improved. My daughter still needed a small bottle three times a day, but we were actively decreasing the amount as she and I both improved at nursing.

"Why don't you go by yourself?" he offered.

The idea enticed me. *Am I allowed to leave her?*

After a bit of ping-pong inside my brain, I made the decision to leave my tiny little responsibility alone with her daddy for the first time so I could do some grocery shopping *by myself*.

I wandered the Trader Joe's aisles feeling like I held a secret no one knew. I felt free.

Some time after my invigorating solo grocery trip, my husband bought a bike trailer and occasionally took the baby on long rides, giving me some space at home so I could nap, enjoy my quiet house, or pay bills in peace. For the first time in months, I was able to breathe deeply.

The climb up the mountain of motherhood became more enjoyable and easier as I leaned into my husband and allowed him to explore the trail of fatherhood. Sharing the responsibility for our sweet new addition allowed us both the space to adjust to the pressure of parenthood.

We continued the parenthood climb by adding two more babies, both boys, in the following four years. We linked arms, put one foot in front of the other and became a one-income, debt-free family. We bought our first house and began homeschooling. Two more babies followed, a girl and a boy, and we moved again. The more we relied on one another through the steep climb, the more base camps we reached; each one providing a new opportunity to acclimate to the diverse challenges that came with raising a family.

It's Friday, which means laundry day. I catch up on some Marco Polo messages while I finish folding the fifth load of laundry of the morning. I check my texts and confirm our babysitter for date night tonight. My oldest daughter saunters into the laundry room to grab her hamper of clean laundry, and two gangly brothers follow behind her carrying their own hampers of laundry to be washed. Laundry day turns my laundry room into Grand Central Station—hampers become trains, arriving dirty, departing clean and folded.

"I'm going to go fold my clothes and put them away," my oldest says nonchalantly as she lifts her hamper with her strong, freckled arms and heads toward her room. "Then can I FaceTime with Zoe so we can work on our book?" Her 12-year-old eyebrows move up and down repeatedly, convincing me that her plan is solid.

"Yes! Go to it!" I say enthusiastically—one less load to stare me down will be a welcome relief.

"Boys! Come back and put your wash in!" I yell as they try to sneak out of the laundry room under the cover of their big sister. They slowly walk back and start dumping their unmentionables into the machine basin.

I turn back to Mt. Laundry once again, but start to hear suspicious bings and beeps behind me, emanating from the washing machine. I move over to stand behind my 10-year-old while showing him, "It's this button, honey. See? Just press it once and wait. Then it'll turn on."

He added the soap by himself this time (a huge win), and I understand how a 10-year-old would be drawn to the sounds produced by a modern washing machine. Having finished his part, he starts to depart, and I remind both him and his brother to finish emptying the dishwasher before they go play.

I take a breath and return to the laundry Everest still in front of me just as my 3-year-old daughter comes rushing into the laundry room from outside. With a skeptical look on her face, she greets me with: "Don't push it, bub." It's a line from one of her favorite Elephant & Piggie books. I lean against the laundry room counter as I give a hearty, genuine laugh. Her 3-year-old experiments with humor and comic timing delight and surprise me. I chase down a hug from her and shoo her back outside so I can, once again, return to epic laundry-folding. My littlest son, still a toddler, tries on and discards every shoe from our stockpile under the laundry room counter. His presence and toddler-chatter is calming to me, even though I'm interrupted frequently to stop him from banging his brother's cowboy boot or my ankle bootie too hard on the tile floor.

*Huh, that's interesting,* I think to myself as I grab another towel off the top of the never-ending mountain. I recall another morning, 12 years ago, when a failed nursing session and the mere presence of Mt. Laundry stopped my breath completely, replacing it with heaving sobs and tearful anxiety. Now, in this current scene, I breathe in deep even though the tasks of motherhood have multiplied exponentially and the number of children has grown to five. *Why am I able to breathe deeply now?*

Acclimation.

My current base camp looks very different from the

first one from long ago. Older children sharing the work of keeping our house running and the energizing opportunities to engage with all five of my children on various levels serve to get my mama-lungs the oxygen they need. Learning to lean on my husband and partner with him through the trenches of parenting has helped lift the weight I originally thought was solely mine to bear. I have adjusted to this new mothering altitude and I can breathe more easily while I continue climbing to the next base camps: mom of teenagers, mom of college kids, mom of married children, empty nest mom, grandma.

"You sad, Mama?" My little guy always notices when my face changes to crying mode. The tears fill my eyes and I grab a clean washcloth from the mountainous pile in front of me. I carefully dry my eyes as I think of all that's to come.

"I'm okay, buddy!" I say. Surprisingly, I *am* okay. I'm not overwhelmed with the daily tasks of mothering or worried about what may lie ahead. I have learned that the present base camp is the best place for me to breathe, to acclimate. I am committed to this journey wholeheartedly, all the way to the very top of the mountain. I pause and take a moment to look out from my vantage point.

The view before me is breathtaking.

# OUR COLLECTIVE STRENGTH

*Bethany McMillon*

I SAT BLEARY-EYED AT THE KITCHEN TABLE. Saturday morning had arrived at last. My coffee was in a ceramic mug, and I was still in my pajamas. Sticky plates from our pancake feast were stacked on the table in front of me. I ignored them as I scrolled through social media. A slow morning at home was just what we needed to settle our souls during a particularly wild season.

I'd recently gone back to full-time teaching, and our weekday pace was frantic. My growing-too-fast boy lounged on the couch with eyes glued to the television. I wished for a moment he'd chosen a different mode of relaxation, but instead of asking him to turn it off, I snuggled in beside him to finish off my coffee.

Instead of cartoons, he chose a documentary featuring animals of the savanna on one of the science channels. Within moments, my eyes, too, were glued to the scene unfolding before us.

119

In the video, a small herd of Cape buffalo meandered along a riverbank when a troop of lions ambushed them. Lions grabbed a baby buffalo as it fell into the water, and the mature buffaloes took off running. I gasped, unable to take my eyes off the chaotic scene on the television. The situation went from bad to worse for the baby as the camera panned to the water. Two beady reptile eyes hovered at the surface. In a blink, I heard a *snap!*

I screamed and grabbed my boy's hand. "Oh, my goodness! Is the baby going to get torn in two?" At which point, he rolled his eyes, saying, "Just watch."

The crocodile had one of the baby's hooves in its mouth and was dragging it into the water. The lions had the baby by the head, yanking in the other direction. Suddenly, the baby popped out of the water with all four legs still intact! But, just as quickly, the lions overcame it! The awful scene was heart-wrenching.

By now, I'd set my coffee mug down and sat perched at the edge of my seat. All of a sudden, the most incredible thing happened: the adult Cape buffaloes charged back into the action zone! This time, the small group was not alone. The entire herd stampeded toward the lions. One of them leaned down to head-butt a lion and sent it flying through the air.

I heard a sound from the baby buffalo, and my jaw dropped: it was *alive!* The buffaloes speared the other lions off the baby. The herd enveloped the baby back into their protection, and the lions scattered.

The video panned away from the scene as the climactic rescue returned to pictures of the tranquil savanna. I stood up, hugged my boy and with a deep breath, I attempted to resume our relaxed Saturday. As I washed plates, I remembered back to a trip we took through a safari park in northern California. While driving through the Cape buffalo area, a guide said these animals were known to attack as a herd to defend each other.

Herds. Villages. Friendships. Our people. In compromising circumstances, the small group ran to round up the rest of the herd because all of them were needed to protect the baby in both the heat of the attack and the aftermath. The herd demonstrated strength in numbers.

When I returned to full-time teaching, I learned how important it is to be part of a strong community. The change was sudden, and my village—my herd—stepped in to care for my family when I felt like the new array of demands on my time might tear me in two. We received prayers and sweet messages. Others stepped in to take care of my boy and to feed our family on nights when the schedule was overfull.

One morning during the first week of school, just as I walked my class out to recess, my phone rang. I didn't want to take a call while I was with my students, so I declined it. But after receiving three consecutive calls within five minutes, I decided it must be important. I flagged down a colleague to watch my class for a moment so I could return the call. Just as someone answered on the other end, I remembered: I'd scheduled a repair person, and in the midst of beginning this new job, I hadn't thought to cancel it! I had no time to drive home and back to school. In a panic, I called for reinforcements. A kind neighbor-friend knew exactly where we kept our spare key. She rearranged her schedule to work from our living room instead of her home office while the repairs were being made. Each minute of help offered by our village gave me life.

I'm continually faced with balancing family demands, pressure at work, and the urge to give time to another ministry to which I feel called. During a recent coffee date, the conversation turned to all the things we juggle as moms. My friends heard the anxiety rise in my voice as I gave details about a specific issue on my mind. Without hesitation, one of them reached across the table, squeezed my hand, and said, "Let's pray about this right now." Everyone lowered their heads and, together, we handed the situation over to God. Even though I'd prayed over the same issue myself countless times, hearing my community pray about my anxious heart changed my perspective. I knew I wasn't alone.

When I'm struggling, I tend to retreat inward. I want to lick my wounds privately and replay conversations in my head. I compare my worst to someone else's best. My friends somehow know this. They know to hem me back into fellowship and surround me with their collective strength. Strength often comes in quiet, small ways—a kind word, a cup of coffee, a prayer, or an afternoon together with our kids.

In Luke 6, Jesus gives one of His most quoted commands: "Do to others as you would have them do to you." Jesus's words give guidance for building community relationships. To create or deepen connection within my community, I can notice a need and work to fill it, speak life-giving words, extend an invitation to spend time together, or even answer the call for a friend's emergency need for a spare key!

Sometimes our people save us from lions, and other times we must be the charging herd ready to protect our own.

Whether they be herds or villages, close or faraway friends, old companions or newest acquaintances, our people are necessary for our survival and strength.

# POSSIBILITIES AND IMPERFECT PROGRESS

*Jennifer Van Winkle*

K
NOCK KNOCK. I peep through the curtains to see the delivery man walking away from my door and back to his van. "Thank you!" I call. He waves his hand, briefly turning back toward me. *Finally, it's here.* I grab the kitchen scissors to slice the packing tape, lifting the cardboard flaps to reveal what I hope will help me make sense of the jumbled mess in my mind: a planning journal.

Leafing through the pages, the possibilities of how I can fill them pulse through my already full mind. *This is going to help so much.* I am constantly thinking about what needs to be done, how to stay one step ahead so as not to be swallowed whole. I reason all of my trouble staying sane and organized is because I don't have a place to collect the thoughts to preserve them from vaporizing into the ether. Pen in hand, I open to the section meant to record SMART goals, and I freeze.

*This is a pen, for goodness' sake.*
*I can't use a pen.*
*A pen is permanent.*
*I can't brain-dump on these pages.*
*Maybe I can find some scratch paper.*

I end up keeping the thoughts inside my already cluttered mind so as not to mar the pristine pages. I hypothesize, theorize, and philosophize about how to artfully capture my thoughts. I am terrified of writing the wrong thing in the wrong way, so I write nothing, save birthdays and anniversaries. All the hope I had of momentum toward clearing my mental clutter dries into one big, misplaced ink spot.

I close the planner in frustration and open another book: an exercise manual. One of the many things on my mental to-do list is exercise—yet another attempt to quiet my perpetually running mind. I flip to the workout scheduled for today.

Burpees.

That infernal exercise makes me look like a complete imbecile. The fitness model, on the other hand, looks amazing. She begins in a perfect push-up position: legs, back, and head in one long, lean line. Each picture displays perfect form and athleticism. She hops effortlessly, bringing her feet forward to land outside of her hands, then shoots high into the air like a rocket. Back down again, hands to the floor, and hops her feet back to the starting point. Bing. Bang. Boom. She makes it look so easy.

I unfurl my purple exercise mat, lace up my shoes, and prepare for the exercise. Physically, my body is warmed up and ready to go, but mentally, I am everywhere but the mat.

Push-up position. *Yikes, my floor is dirty.*

Feet hop forward to meet hands. *Did I defrost the chicken?* Jump up, arms reaching to the sky. "Mom, where is my sock?" *Kinda busy.*

Squat down, hands to the floor. *Gosh, this is so hard.* Feet jump back into a push-up. *When will this be over?!* Feet hop forward to meet hands. *Why am I doing this?* Jump up, arms reaching. *I can do this. One more minute.*

I start with good form, but it deteriorates as I continue. My push-up resembles more of a mountain shape with every rep, my rear end inching higher and higher like a periscope searching for ally ships come to rescue. Heaving and panting, I count each squeak of my sneakers against the hardwood floor. Each one is a little closer to my new goal of stopping this hellish exercise.

Most of the time, when I fixate on my failures, they push me into paralysis. I wish I could do this exercise like the fitness model, with poise and power, but I just want to continue to the next move or give up entirely. Rare is the instance in which I continue to push through, tolerating imperfection. I am fallible, unlike that model or the blank planner pages. But something changes mentally as I continue—things are getting clearer.

Mid-jump, I realize I'm still exercising; I haven't given up yet. It may not be pretty, but something is better than nothing. I may complain about how hard this is and how I wish I were doing anything else on God's green earth, but I am still moving. Even with all the kicking and screaming and atrocious form, I am farther down the road than when I started. I trade physical agility for mental clarity.

I put myself through this exercise a couple times a week, motivated partly by vanity. Over time, I have been surprised to realize I look forward to a workout, not for a six-pack or flat tummy, but because when I do something physical with my body, it offers my brain a chance to let go of perfectionism. Imperfect exercise makes space in my mind for imperfect movement toward every other goal in my life.

When I exercise, it is time for my mind to listen and not do the talking. I tune in to how my body feels, pay attention to what is physically challenging, and appreciate what isn't as hard today as it was yesterday. When I stretch out a sore muscle and gently breathe deeper into the discomfort, I acknowledge the underappreciated things my body does every day. My muscles seem thankful for the opportunity to work. My lungs are grateful to do their job. It feels good to have blood pumping through my veins, and each drop of sweat is a hard-earned nugget of euphoria, valuable because it is rare in my days spent giving my all to my young family.

When my mind begins to reel off course and I begin to think way too much about the order in which I should shower, do laundry, write a grocery list, and the like, moving my body is often the missing component needed to restore balance to my well-being.

I exercise to clear the mental fog and break up the cycle of overthinking everything. Incidentally, I have found that when I offer my mind this kind of break each day, I end up having some of my best ideas. Like finding a dollar bill in the pocket of a pair of jeans I haven't worn (or washed) for a while, these good ideas are given to me without searching or striving hard to find them. Just as a passenger in a car gets to relax and take in the scenery while the driver remains alert to events unfolding on the road, my brain enjoys being the passenger instead of white-knuckling the steering wheel of decision-making all the time. When my brain rests, creative thought comes bubbling up.

I love that this very physical practice fuels my creative life. Establishing the habit of doing something physical every day helps me be a better mother. I give my children a positive example of prioritizing a healthy lifestyle, even though I may look silly and sort of pathetic as I do it. Knowing I am helping to instill in them healthy habits for their lifetime pushes me to work harder—both figuratively and literally—as they enjoy handing me heavier weights during my workouts. "Do it again with this weight, Mom…it's heavier!" *You got it, Coach.*

So I lace up my sneakers every day. It is worthwhile for me to put up with looking like a dork with a periscope booty. I keep showing up for these workouts that help center me. I bring every last ounce of determination to let my mind rest and allow my body to take control and move. Tomorrow I will be capable of more because of what I struggle through today. It's not perfect, but something is better than nothing. I am stronger today than I was yesterday.

Burpees, you bloody beasts, I'll see you tomorrow. I've written it in my new planner, with a pen.

# SHATTERING SCARCITY

*Mary Kate Brown*

M IRACULOUSLY, our morning was going according to plan. We were up on time, the kids were already wearing their Christmas pajamas, and our gifts were ready at the door. The only thing left to do was load the car and go.

It was still dark outside—we wanted to get on the road as soon as possible so we could join family for breakfast. I began ushering my sleepy-eyed (yet excited) daughters through the dimly lit kitchen to make sure they used the bathroom before we left while Brian loaded our things into the van. Suddenly, I heard a muffled *BOOM* and *CRASH*. I paused for a short moment, not assuming the worst, and continued with the task of making sure every kid had a turn on the potty.

My husband burst through the door breathless, red in the face, and announced, "The window just shattered." Visibly shaken, he explained that the struts on the rear liftgate of our minivan gave out, and the door slammed down (thankfully missing his head), shattering our rear window. *So much for being on time.*

Inside I fumed. *Why this? Why now?* I calmly redirected my kids to watch a cartoon so I could escape to the shower. I reassured them that Christmas was not cancelled, but self-ishly I wished it had been. Beneath the hot, running water, I felt too upset to even cry. Family dynamics alone were enough to make holiday plans stressful, and our broken window was the final straw after a month of similar mishaps that added to a burden we felt might actually crush us.

Our car wouldn't start. The indoor furnace fan went out. The outdoor wood-boiler furnace fan went out at the very same time, complicating the task of heating our home in the middle of a Michigan December. A drain pipe in the basement kept freezing and flooding our utility room. The sum of these and several other unexpected expenses meant, once again, Brian and I could not afford gifts for each other this year. For the first time, we couldn't afford them for our kids, either. With each unexpected repair or mishap, we saw more dollar signs in the negative. We felt *awesome.*

Ten years prior, as hopeful and naive 20-year-old newly-weds, we survived on weekly paychecks from our respective part-time work. I was still in school, and Brian was a sub-stitute teacher. We only had ourselves to worry about then, but I can still remember the sinking feeling I'd have when we'd go to buy groceries. We didn't have any negotiable bills—no cable, no subscriptions, no fancy smartphones. Just the boring essentials like water, rent, and electric. We didn't go out on dates very frequently, and we both took any opportunity offered to make some extra cash—nannying, dog-sitting, wrapping Christmas gifts for a family I worked for, or shampooing carpets in professors' offices on our college campus. We hustled but barely made ends meet.

Returning from one of our shopping trips, I was near tears as I walked from my car to our back door. Sure, we had groceries for this week, but what about next? I happened to glance down at the garden planted by one of the tenants in the basement apartment and noticed a small sculpture of two cupped hands with a bird helping itself to seeds nestled inside them. A stone inscription below read: *"By His hands we are fed."* I felt encouraged by that tiny inscription, and I would acknowledge it with a smile each time I brought my groceries home from that day forward. Little did I know how much I'd learn this truth over the years.

Even after that newlywed season, we seldom had any financial margin. The same year our first child was born, Brian moved from a management position with a small company to an art teaching position at a small private school; with it came an even smaller salary. I struggled with this job change because it felt like we were taking a step in the wrong direction. We didn't doubt he was called to this job in this season, and even if we wanted to ignore that call, all other job leads ran cold. During the six years he worked as a teacher, I had some serious relearning to do. The fear I carried with me related to finances only pointed to a deeper heart issue I'd not yet dealt with: I was afraid God wouldn't provide for our family's needs.

When we found ourselves in the position of having to trust God instead of the numbers in our bank account, we became receivers of His unique provision time and time again. "God, we trust you," became our continual declaration.

We grew to understand that no matter how much income we had, if our hearts did not know our Father as our provider, we'd *always* feel like it wasn't enough. We asked God to help us live generously, despite what our bank account looked like. For a good number of years, our budget was so tight it legitimately made no sense on paper, but we never went without. Even with little, we learned what it meant to give joyfully.

On one occasion, Brian confidently declared, "I believe God wants us to double our giving every month." I felt fear start to rise up inside of me, but I simply replied, "Okay, let's do it." I resolved that God's kingdom doesn't operate the way ours does. And even if we stopped giving altogether, I still wouldn't feel like we had enough, so why not just give more? For every month we doubled our giving that year, God somehow returned to us what we'd given and then some. It was a unique season where God showed us the beauty of keeping our hands open, ready to give and receive. We didn't want to be like a vault made to store and protect our resources, but like a funnel through which they could flow.


Our current season is unlike any we've experienced before. We actually have a budget that makes sense on paper and we live in a home of our own. We've learned to place our trust in His faithfulness, not solely in our own capabilities. We're learning to steward well the blessings we've been entrusted with. *By His hands we are fed.*

I have walked too far with God to doubt Him now. He's proven His faithfulness too many times for me to think a shattered car window would be our financial undoing. His provision has covered our needs in the past; surely our window, our furnaces, and our drain pipe aren't beyond His ability to provide. The fruit of the spirit is joy, and it is peace.

I finished showering, took a nap, and had a cup of coffee. Our parents picked us up, and we shared a late breakfast with them that morning. Christmas wasn't cancelled. My burning anger over all of the situations from December ultimately subsided, and with it, the temptation to fear we wouldn't have enough money to fix all the things and pay our bills.

After breakfast, my kids opened their presents. I watched while reflecting on a conversation I had with my mother-in-law just a week prior, when she asked, "What do you and Brian want for Christmas?" "Honestly," I answered, "we would like to buy the girls each a gift." It was totally unconventional, but thanks to PayPal and Amazon Prime, three packages arrived just days before Christmas. Each of our girls opened their gifts from us Christmas morning: a doll, a telescope, and another doll that looked like a newborn baby. They were as overjoyed and ecstatic as they'd have been if we surprised them with a trip to Disney.

My heart swelled with gratitude as my kids squealed with delight over their presents. I realized, once again, that I was the recipient of God's unique provision.

# AT THE END OF MYSELF

*Emily Sue Allen*

My house is quiet—kids tucked in, baby nursed and passed out in the bassinet. My husband is beside me in the bed, engrossed in a sci-fi novel on his Kindle. With a flick of my finger, I scroll social media to check in with friends and acquaintances. It's an ordinary Thursday night.

I'm still coming down from the day. Chaos, commotion, enthusiasm, and energy—my children have no shortage of any of the above. I am taking a full, deep breath when it hits me.

At first, a tingly sensation floods my whole body. Then a jolt of terror explodes through the center of my chest. I am all at once, instantly, *not okay*. My heart races, and I am filled with a heavy and foreboding dread. I might die.

Like, *right now*.

I spring out of bed and race to the bathroom, my insides churning, my bladder feeling suddenly weak. I breathe hard and choke back tears and attempt a full body assessment.

*What is going on?* I have no answers.

I think through the possibilities. *Do I have a blood clot again?* I recall last year's life-threatening clot lodged in my lung. *Is it my heart?...* Or no—*maybe it's my kidneys failing.* I am spinning. It's been maybe 60 seconds since I was peacefully stretched out in my bed.

I try to reason myself to stability.

*Emily, you're fine. You're not going to die. You don't have a blood clot. If you do, you'll know. You're familiar with those sensations, which are not like these.*

I return to my bed and don't say a word to my husband. I'm afraid he'll look at me like I'm a total weirdo (which, let's be honest, I am—but not because of this). I still feel tingly and strange. He turns out the light and snores his way to the morning, but me? I thrash restlessly for hours, unable to calm down, unable to sleep.

It was a normal day, a normal month even, full of garden-variety challenges I was used to navigating as a mother with many children. I truly hadn't felt it coming: my first anxiety attack. It was the first of many in the following months, each surprise attack a direct threat to my well-established reputation for being a steady, capable, available person.

*Terror* is the best word I can use to describe it. I felt weak, uncertain, and unable to rescue myself from whatever this new, unwelcome experience was. I thought terrible thoughts, and what-ifs curled their sharp nails around my thin places. I did not understand what was happening to me, and once the symptoms started escalating, I was powerless to stop them.

I tried keeping the extent of my fear under wraps, and pushed through as best as I could, but after a month of

anxiety attacks happening every few days, I landed in a full
meltdown one day.

I was clearing dishes and hanging up coats when,
suddenly, I was leveled. I dropped to the couch in uncon-
trollable sobs. Everything was fine, until it wasn't.

A kid asked me, "Mom, can I have a string cheese?"

And another, "Mama, is it okay to put on a show for the
little kids?"

Each time, I waved my hand without looking up, a
gesture meant to say, *Figure it out. I can't answer you right
now.* I couldn't even give a simple response to a straightfor-
ward question.

Then I cried harder because there was no way to "be a
good mom" in this condition.

After that, I was hit with anxiety/overwhelm/burnout
or whatever this was, on a regular basis. Every time, I was
bewildered by the intensity of the experience.

Early on, I mentioned it to my doctor. He was
focused on other pressing health concerns and dismissed the
anxiety altogether. I mean, I hadn't exactly gone in with an
articulate way to describe what I was experiencing. When I
realized these episodes were untenable for me, I knew
counseling was the next right step.

My counselor tells me I've come to the end of myself,
and most women arrive here somewhere around the age
of 40. Just a little ahead of schedule at 36 years old, I'm
here. I mean, my experience is made up of multiple layers—
postpartum depression, ongoing health anxiety in the
aftermath of a near-death experience, and latent grief from
earlier in my life—but this "pile-up" experience is apparently not unique to me.

I've known for a few decades counseling might benefit me, given all the things I've experienced. However, in my twenties and early thirties, I was hell-bent on figuring things out myself without anyone's help. I'm a fighter. Even if it meant taking the long, winding, treacherous road, I've always chosen the DIY way of things, for good or for bad.

I told more than one friend I was trying to untangle a web of things I couldn't see or understand. I have thrashed. I have cried. I have gotten still and quiet and withdrawn. I have hated every minute of being completely out of control of my internal and overall well-being.

I'm not jazzed about my well-kept threads unraveling into a tangled mess before my eyes, without my permission. I've been embarrassed, uncomfortable, and at some moments, downright terrified of what is happening to me during these anxiety attacks. However, I have also come to realize God is at work in me, specifically in this weakness. He has allowed this unraveling for a real and important purpose.

I have not arrived at an "all better" spot. A few months of counseling have brought me enormous gifts and breakthroughs in areas I didn't know I needed them. It's like God has allowed a "light momentary afflic-tion" (2 Corinthians 4:17-18), which, though painful-ly crushing, is ushering a deep and profound healing in areas of my soul I didn't know needed such attention.

I would never have chosen this season, but I see good and beautiful things coming out of it. I have never been more convinced of God's personal and intimate love for me as I have been through this experience. He is not absent. Details surrounding my care, emotional and physical sup-port from my community, the compassion of my husband, the growth in my kids to contribute to our daily household routines are all enough to regularly draw tears of gratitude.

I have been profoundly humbled in this season—much more than I ever signed up for. I've learned that being at the end of myself is not a commentary on my value or worth. Even when I have nothing left to give (and admittedly well before I've given anything), I am loved by God, chosen before the foundation of the world, as He says in Ephesians 1:4.

At the end of myself, I put my tired certainty to rest—all the answers I've been eager to supply—and let my questions hang in the air with a foundation of hope. I trust Jesus is before all things, and in Him all things hold together, even me (Colossians 1:17). While I feel like I'm breaking apart and unraveling, He has me in the palm of His hand—this may be the only thing I am completely certain of.

This experience has been painful and wretched in plenty of ways, but in the midst of it, I've found freedom from the pressure to perform. I have shaken off the notion that to do important things in the world, I need to draw attention to myself, build my audience, and push doors open. If the Lord goes before me, I don't need to lead the way. I'm here on His errands, to do His will, and He will make a way for each and every thing He calls me to.

At the end of myself, I no longer have to carry the weight of the world on my shoulders. I can't anyway, even if I want to. I've had to set that crushing boulder down in order to enter God's rest, which He gives generously to those who will trade their pride and self-sufficiency for it. I can't have the rest without the surrender.

I am in a paradoxical, vulnerable place where I desperately, feverishly crave a way out of pain and discomfort, but where I have also learned God is able to hold me. He is able to bring the care and support I need, and He has. To count all the ways would require many volumes of books. If He ever opens the doors for me to write those books, you can bet I will.

At the end of myself, I can finally acknowledge my days (each one of them) are in God's hands. I am from the earth, a finite, regular mom, formed and sustained by a love beyond anything I can grasp.

I find myself swimming in grace—grace I could not know if I were not at the end of myself.

# PART IV

# I DON'T WANT MY
# PRE-BABY BODY BACK

*Lindsey Cornett*

I LOOKED DOWN AT MY PURPLE MAT AND STARED AT THE space between my two hands.

"Hands shoulder-width apart," the instructor said, and I adjusted slightly.

Just a few days before, I learned my second baby was a boy, and it seemed like as good a time as any to attend a prenatal yoga class—my first yoga class of any kind. We had set our intentions (I chose "joy") and were now on all fours, progressing through a series of cat/cow poses. I tried to smoothly move in time with my breathing and the barely perceptible music. Then the instructor said, "Let's connect with our bodies now."

I paused, throwing off my rhythm, as a thought ran through my head. *Have I ever done that before?*

"Feel the ground beneath you," she continued. "Can you feel it beneath each finger? Beneath your palms?

Beneath your knees?" She then encouraged us to push into the ground under each toe, our heels, and the balls of our feet.

It was so simple and so revelatory, like a newborn's first smile: simple, commonplace, reflexive, and yet wonderful. As I pressed into my mat with each extremity, my body and the world met each other, perhaps for the first time. Had I ever paid such attention to my breathing? Had I ever asked the whole of my body's movements to come into rhythm with one another, as if dancing? Could I stop to feel the ground below me, connecting my soul and my heart and my body?

As a child, I learned my body was uncoordinated. In a fourth-grade unit on bicycle safety, I was the only student off to the side with the P.E. coach, attempting to learn to ride without training wheels. (Unsuccessfully, I'll add.) As a seventh grader, I tried out for the middle school volleyball team and just barely made the cut, only to see my serving skills actually diminish as the season wore on, despite almost-daily team practices.

In high school, I learned my body made me a target. During back-to-school shopping, my mom and I looked for the most modest clothing (some of which my dad still deemed not quite modest enough). Even that failed to shield me from unwanted advances, snide remarks, and uncomfortable attention. In my sophomore-year history class, a boy threw small bits of paper down my shirt while we sat working on a group project. I looked to the teacher as if to say, "What should I do about this?" He looked at me and said, "You should be ashamed of yourself, young lady." I wasn't sure what to be ashamed of besides my body.

In college, I learned my body was confusing. My scoliosis continued to worsen for no apparent reason— "idiopathic," the orthopedic surgeon called it—and while my peers spent the summer after sophomore year interning and studying abroad, I spent it on my parents' couch recovering from spinal fusion. A few years later, I began having trouble eating certain foods; my bite was askew, and my retainer no longer fit. X-rays and MRIs showed deteriorating joints in my jaw, but follow-up tests revealed no cause. To this day, my jaw hangs open awkwardly, but with none of the TMJ or headaches the doctors told me to expect.

All along, I have felt my body couldn't be trusted.

As a lifelong perfectionist, I tend to ignore and avoid anything that doesn't come naturally or for which I lack confidence. I quit gymnastics lessons because I was afraid of flipping over the uneven bars. I didn't show up to my AP Calculus exam. I shelved my book-writing project for over a year. Similarly, I've mostly ignored my body. It didn't perform or behave as I expected, and I've never been comfortable with unreliability and failures. I pushed through pain and worked past tired. I've acquiesced to cravings and avoided doctors. I have walked through the world like a disembodied mind and heart.

When the time finally came for my second son to be born, my doctor stood at the foot of the bed with a nurse and two residents by her side. I breathed. I counted. My body created and sustained a rhythm all its own. The time came, and I bore down.

"She's a good pusher," my doctor said.

She said it to the nurse in a hushed voice; I don't believe she meant for me to hear.

I remember very little from that day because clouds of

postpartum depression eventually descended and drove out many of my memories of Leo's first year of life. I remember the boldly patterned glasses of the medical resident, a nurse laying my husband onto a couch after he passed out, another nurse counting the minutes between my contractions, and those four words: *She's a good pusher.*

For so many years, I lacked the strength, coordination, and stamina required for any physical task I encountered. Both times it became clear my labor would need to be induced, it seemed to confirm for me that somehow my body didn't know what it was doing. And yet there—in that most crucial moment—my body knew what to do?

My body knew what to do.

Carrying and delivering my children brought me in tune with my own body. It's only in recent years that I have learned to track my mood and up my Vitamin D when necessary, noticed coffee after 4:00 pm makes me jittery and unable to sleep, realized my knee swells with alarming regularity once a month.

When my own well-being was all that hung in the balance, ignoring potential problems and ailments was easier than addressing them. But ignoring my body during pregnancy meant ignoring the needs of another person for whose nourishment and sustenance I was responsible. I've heard that a pregnancy is the surest way to drastically change a person's bad habits—whether drinking or smoking or just plain negligence—and I believe it. What is permissible in isolation is no longer acceptable in relationship.

That second baby will start Pre-K soon. I am still not keen on exercising and I have not become an athlete. When our family purchased a gym membership, I took advantage of the free childcare but spent most of my time sipping coffee and reading in the lobby. And yet I feel at home in my body; I am more dedicated to listening to her cues and I trust her to carry me through.

My pre-baby body was good too, of course. She was not at all unreliable or untrustworthy—that was my fear and insecurity talking. And she would have been whole and wholly good even if I had never conceived or carried or delivered a baby, but birth was the means by which I learned what I needed to know.

Motherhood has given me my body for the first time. The power of connection with my unborn children and the challenge and fulfillment of delivering them into the world—the intermingling of body and heartbeat, breath and blood—transformed my body and gave her new life as she did the same for another. I've learned to love her—my pre-baby and post-baby body too. There is no going back.

# PREVAILING STRENGTH

*Lynne Patti*

THE SWEAT IS STREAMING DOWN MY BACK, but the sun is welcoming, not angry. My backpack is chafing a bit due to the sunburn I have achieved as we hike the side of this canyon. There is a satisfaction that comes with the hard work of exercising, of putting to use muscles that haven't seen action for a while. I plod along, one foot in front of the other, longing for the rest ahead when we reach the top. My husband's pocket spits out lyrics from *Hamilton*, our soundtrack to this family adventure. The familiar music keeps rhythm and helps me move forward despite being winded.

We have already hiked two and a half miles up to a waterfall. Hidden among the gracious sycamores and oaks, the view is a wonderful reward for the hard work of hiking up. My spirit is refreshed from a momentary pitstop for snacks and a long gaze at the waterfall. Now, as the smell of lemongrass wafts across my consciousness now and again, we are headed down, back to the car. The sycamores and oaks that flourish by the waterfall have now been replaced with generic desert shrubbery and a dusty path. We have a mile and half remaining until we're back in our minivan and immersed in some A/C for the long drive home.

Earlier today, back home at our kitchen table with coffee and confidence in hand, we thought a family hike would be just perfect. Five miles round-trip seemed totally doable. Presently, my oldest child lags as she looks for lizards, my oldest boy is red-faced and forlorn, the next boy is quickly losing the pep in his step, and the baby is peacefully sleeping in the carrier on Daddy's back. I am seriously rethinking our kitchen-table confidence.

I look at my 5-year-old son and realize he's not going to make it.

"You've got this, buddy! You've done so well today! I'm so proud of you!"

He continues to walk slowly, head down, red cheeks hiding in the shadow of his exhaustion.

I assess the unfolding events and realize no amount of encouragement will get him to continue step, step, stepping down to the bottom of the canyon where we've parked our car. *He's done.* The last thing I want to do is carry another human for the remaining mile plus, but with our littlest baby in the Ergo on Daddy, my back is the only one available. I hand Daddy the backpack I've been carrying and take my son by the arms.

"Jump!" I say as I swing him up on my back. My hands find each other behind me under his little bottom. I tell myself to settle in because this one won't be hiking again today.

At first, it's easy. Heading downhill and already sweaty, there isn't much I need to worry about. But even the easy 50

154

pounds of a 5-year-old old will test a mother's back. As we sway and bob down the mountain, I feel his muscles grow slack—a sure sign he's fallen asleep. Now my commitment must remain strong. With a sleeping child on my back, I cannot give up. He has no thought of my strength or ability to endure, only his own exhaustion. I smile a bit as I consider his total dependence on my strength.

A cool breeze brushes my hair against my reddened face and I think of his face, set like steel during a recent disciplinary time-out session. First-time obedience has never been a part of this kid's playing deck. He's landed in the proverbial prison of childhood—the time-out seat—more times than any of my other children. He often resolutely resists correction and fiercely fights back at the slightest provocation.

However, just as I felt him slip into sweet rest on our hike down the canyon, his stubbornness during our disciplinary interactions soon also melts away. I've learned he *wants* the conflict, seeks it out, even, in order to bring us closer together. It's how he builds intimacy. I don't always understand it, but the strength of my resolve as a mother in these scenarios, the strength it takes me to stick with him and not abandon him, to support him even in his rage, reminds me of the strength of my back now as I usher him down to the finish line.

My back. It aches sometimes. It's usually tense in one spot or another, from nursing, scrubbing, holding, dish-doing, or bending over to pick up errant toys. I don't often think about the aches. They seem to come with the motherhood package. But now, as I bear the weight of my boy, I think about my back and the strength it wields.

Strength to hold me up.

Strength to give good, strong hugs.

Strength to bring laundry upstairs or down.

Strength to bend and scoop up a crying baby in the night.

Strength to walk for miles and miles in a marathon.

Strength to labor and deliver babies.

Strength to weep for the babies I miscarried.

Strength to let go and lean into my husband for his strength.

Strength to sit next to a sick child, making sure they fall asleep.

Strength to piggyback my children up to their beds for pure fun.

We are nearing the parking area, and I realize I've walked for over a mile with my little guy still asleep on my back. My husband yells back to me, "Wow, Supermom, how are you doing?" I chuckle and say, "I'm fine," because *I am*. Am I tired? YES! Am I sweatier than before? Also, yes! Do I regret that we took this hike, or that it was ultimately up to me to help my son reach the destination? Not for one second.

When I reached the travailing part of the hike, I didn't have the option to sit down and give up. I found grit and resolve within me to draw my weary son up—nearer to my heart—to carry him along with me, *and I kept going*. My back is strong, like my love, and this brief moment is one of a thousand other moments of motherhood that illuminate just how strong I am.

# HOW I QUIT STRUGGLING WITH MY WEIGHT

*Robin Chapman*

WELL, SHE'S A LITTLE HEAVIER THAN I LIKE TO SEE for her length. Let's talk about some strategies to handle this. Obesity is a serious health issue, so we want to nip it in the bud."

I was present at this conversation, but I have no memory of it. I only know the bare details my mom told me. I was the pudgy "she" in question.

I was 8 weeks old.

My mom, a first-timer at 28, took in the information Dr. Maples was giving. He had letters after his name; she had only been parenting for two months. Her gut said I was a baby and ought to be fed when I was hungry, but he had the experience to *know*. She did what I would have done in the same situation: she listened to the friendly, grandfatherly man in the white coat who treated hundreds of babies a year.

When he gave this advice in the early '80s, the "obesity epidemic" was just entering the collective consciousness. The majority of newborns had been fed formula for a couple decades, and breastfed babies like me followed a different growth curve, so I seemed chubbier than I "should be." And if "nipping it in the bud" was an option, he was certainly doing his best. I mean, 2 months old. I didn't even know where my hands were. High five to Dr. Maples for early prevention!

Reality worked out differently. The early diet did not, in fact, prevent anything. By my calculations, it likely *caused* the very thing he was trying to prevent. I can't really fault the pediatrician or my mother for doing their best, but these early choices set off a series of biological and neurological coping mechanisms that persist today and aren't doing me any good. It's obvious (now) that putting a newborn on a restricted-calorie diet because of weight is not, perhaps, medically sound.

I don't struggle with my weight anymore. Oh, I'm still squarely in "obese" territory, where I've been for (apparently) my entire life. But, in addition to having a high BMI, I'm also the healthiest I've ever been. I've learned the two aren't mutually exclusive, even from medical or scientific standpoints, whatever the multi-gazillion-dollar fitness industry wants me to believe. My weight is mostly an inconvenience now. The world is made for people smaller than I am. Chairs, bathroom stalls, zipline courses, clothes...all are made for someone at least a little bit lighter or less...abundant. That's annoying. But "annoying" is as far as it goes. Most days, my size no longer feels connected to my worth.

When Jenna, my firstborn, was small, I would sit cross-legged with her on our dingy living-room carpet in the patch of sunlight from our picture window, marveling at her round belly and thigh rolls, the creases on her wrists and ankles, the dimples on her hands where I expected to see knuckles. I was struck by how adorable her chubbiness was, how perfect she would be regardless of size.

I knew in my spirit that my value wasn't in how I look or what I do, but my brain had never gotten the memo. I spent enough time in '90s youth group subculture to spit out "I find my identity in Jesus!" in my sleep, but it never *felt* true. Holding my seconds-old, still-grayish, cone-headed, ET-looking newborn solidified it in my heart: Jenna is a miracle, by virtue of nothing besides her existence. By extension, we all are. *Even I am a miracle—body, mind, and spirit.* I knew I needed to match my opinion of my body with the one I wanted her to have of hers, which was going to require some shifts in my mindset. What stories was I telling myself about the acceptability of my body? What stories did I want to pass on to her?

Nowadays, I focus on gratitude for what my body does. I can heft two kids, a diaper bag, and a week's worth of groceries up a flight and a half of steps in a single trip. (Why I'm so intent on doing it in a single trip is a question for another day.) Speaking of kids, my body grew four of them from scratch. Then it somehow transported those children, who each had weights similar to respectable bowling balls, from the inside of me to the outside of me. It continued to produce the sole sustenance for said babies for several months and supplemental nourishment for a year beyond that. I can be up with a barfing baby for several hours and still make it to Starbucks by 6:00 am to write this essay

159

before my husband leaves for work. And since I mentioned my husband, well…he's not complaining. Not once in 15 years, bless him. My body does plenty for me. It's freaking amazing.

I'm learning to treat my body kindly, like I'd treat a friend. I even refer to it as a "she" just to remind myself to be gentle. This morning, I caught a glimpse of her in the mirror, in all her naked, squishy glory. My first impulse was to hate the way she looks, like she's wearing a mostly-deflated sumo suit, but then I caught her eyes—the kind ones with the lines forming from years of laughing—and smiled. I would not ever once in a million years take a glance at a friend and tell her, "Eew. Your belly inflated and deflated a few times. I know you've tried to do something about it, but you should try harder." I wouldn't even think it. But I have directed those exact words and a thousand variations of them at this sweet woman in the mirror.

I spent three decades trying to loathe her into acceptability. That worked exactly zero times. I could punish myself by starving, exercising to injury, feeling the constant discomfort of too-small clothing, or all of those simultaneously, but (surprise!) none of it ever actually made me smaller. Strangely, the only thing that's affected my weight at all has been ignoring it. I leave the scale alone and simply eat what feels good in my body, exercise because it gives me energy, and dress in clothes that fit, because that's the compassionate way to treat a human.

Dr. Maples mentioned supposed infantile obesity shortly after the birth of each of my younger sisters, but my mom stopped listening. She came into her own as a mother—she let all the rest of her babies grow however they were going to grow, trusting that her gut would help her do right by them. And I've come into my own as well. I don't struggle with my weight anymore—I allow intuition to guide my choices too. I'm healthy, strong, content. My abundant size no longer keeps me from an abundant life.

# FROM CHAOS TO QUIET

*Bethany McMillon*

DELICIOUS CAMPFIRE SMOKE FILLED THE AIR AND covered my clothes. The air was cool for a summer night, and the inky black country sky stretched as far as I could see. Stars like pinpricks of bright lights winked above. I sat perched on a log surrounding the orange glow, with legs stretched out before the flames. I stared into the blaze and listened to the quiet strum of a guitar and my youth leader's words.

"You are your truest self when it is quiet—in the night before you go to sleep or in the morning as you wake. That is where God will meet you. The place where you are still and quiet."

I soaked in the words and wondered how that could be possible when I didn't like the quiet—or the alone. Because inside, my mind churned with the anxieties of fitting in, meeting expectations, and growing up.

Years later, I sat curled up in the corner of our living

room—legs folded under me in our green paisley chair, a warm coffee mug in my hand. In the predawn darkness, a single reading lamp lit the room. Only the snoring dog and the crinkling of pages in my Bible as I turned them broke the silence.

This peaceful start to my days has become a treasure, a balm to my busy life. The quiet is a welcome reprieve. I have learned to love the stillness.


The change was gradual. I returned home from the thoughtful moment at the campfire and surrounded myself with the commotion of teenage life. I fought against solitude by filling my calendar with social events and school and, later, work. I turned up the music, switched on the television, or got out of the house instead of allowing the quiet to settle the noise.

As a young mom, I worked full time. Peace and quiet were rare. Saturday mornings, when my husband was out of the house and my growing boy was napping, I'd craft. As I placed paintbrush to wood, scissors to paper, photographs to books, my mind relaxed in the peaceful silence and drifted into quiet worship. I'd whisper prayers, hum hymns, and simply be still.

I noticed something about those moments. Instead of wanting to fill them with noise, I relished the quiet.

Now, my growing boy is taller than me. Our weekly schedule is still full. There are no more nighttime feedings or nap times or toddler playdates. Now, there are sports and school and friends. I no longer fight the idea of being alone in the quiet. Instead, I look for ways to fit it in.

Peace. Margins. This idea of "un-rushing"—purposefully slowing down, so I'm not barreling through life at breakneck speed—beckons my heart. Over and over, it calls me to still my body, so in turn, I can allow God's mercies to still my soul. I want, as the Psalmist did, to "seek peace and pursue it" (Psalm 34:14).

When I notice my calendar is too full, feel my shoulders begin to rise, feel my breath become shallow, feel my my mind race, I consider one of these ways to turn toward the quiet:

I take a walk. I focus on just my steps and my thoughts. My mind and heart revel in the quiet time, my body in the activity.

I visit with a friend. Eye contact, proximity, and voices impact how close we feel to someone. Instead of scrolling social media, I set up a time to meet up with a friend—in person.

I consciously slow my body. I focus on my senses, noticing the things I see, hear, smell. Inhale. Exhale. I pull my shoulders down, straighten my back, and lift my head. I smile. By taking control of my body in this way, I can reverse my stress response.

I pause before moving to the next thing. I take a minute, during errands or before I get out of my car at work or home, to take a deep breath. For just a moment, I relish the quiet and add breathing space to the rush of life.

I praise God for the things He's done. Like the leper in chapter 17 of the Gospel of Luke, I am learning to notice and honor God's work, remembering to double back to thank Him instead of racing forward in life. I'm learning to fall facedown, be still, and thank Jesus for teaching me to find Him in the quiet.

The soft gray of daybreak signals it is time to begin the day, and I hear both my husband and son begin to stir. I close my Bible, switch off the lamp and remember my youth leader's words: "You are your truest self when it is quiet." The memory of that night at the campfire still rises often as I fall asleep or as I wake. Now, I treasure the time to meet God here.

# GO GET HIM, TIGER

*Jennifer Van Winkle*

H E'S LIGHTING THE CANDLES. In an instant, the bottom falls out of the day filled with feuding preschoolers and a fearless acrobat toddler, and suddenly I remember I am a woman—not just a mom, but a real, attractive woman. He sidles up to me as I wash the last of the dinner dishes at the sink, places his hands tenderly on my hips, and whispers in my ear.

"I think you're sexy."

Me. In my apron strings, top knot falling out, still not back to my pre-pregnancy weight. Me.

I turn and give a knowing smile as I saunter to the bathroom—feeling around the dark walls of my mind, trying to flip a switch. I wish there was an easy way to change my mood into one more conducive to the unfolding situation. There are no switches to be found.

*I guess I'll have to do this the hard way.*

I look at myself alone in the mirror, my Sonicare dispatching plaque from my teeth, while I do battle with monsters in my head. I struggle to shut out their loud voices tempting me to avoid an intimate encounter with my husband. *La La La La La!* I press my fingers into my ears and shut my eyes tight and strain to hear the quiet, small voice of love thumping ever onward in my heart.

I can see candlelight flickering from our darkened bedroom, dancing faintly in the hallway, kindled of whispered desire. Tension rises in my shoulders as I contemplate letting him down easy per the monsters' suggestion. Just as quickly, the voice in my heart breaks in to speak truth.

Monsters: I don't want to tonight.

Heart: That is what you said last night.

Monsters: I just don't feel like it.

Heart: Why not?

Monsters: I don't know...It's just a more comfortable idea to crawl into bed and go to sleep.

Heart: Life is too short, you know, to just settle for being unconscious next to a man like him...the man you've chosen. YOUR man.

Me (the final decider): You're right. Time to put my game face on. He'll never know what hit him.

Heart: Go get him, Tiger.

Monsters, zero. Me, more wins than may be appropriate to mention in polite company.


It hasn't always been this way. For a portion of our ten-year marriage, I held my husband at arm's length, apprehensive to show him the real me. I worried if I exposed my most vulnerable self, if my husband really knew me, he might not like me. There were many aspects of myself I felt were substandard, ugly, and downright embarrassing.

I had a warped perspective of beauty, formed when I

was an impressionable girl. It seemed to me women were attractive only if they resembled the ones featured in calendars hanging on toolboxes in a mechanic's shop. I assumed these sexualized images of women must be the universal desire of all men, my husband included. I couldn't picture myself as one of those women, scantily-clad and stiletto-wearing, sprawled over a freshly waxed muscle car, and concluded I was not going to be attractive to my husband since my belly was jelly-like. If I were to lay over the hood of a car, it would look less like "sexy" and more like I was being arrested.

Being rejected by the one to whom I was entirely devoted was the worst thing I could imagine. So I played defense. Under the guise of self-protection, I expertly deflected affectionate advances, completely unaware of any other strategy.

I used all the standard excuses: I'm too tired. I don't feel beautiful. It's too late tonight; maybe tomorrow. I sidestepped his advances by changing the focus of conversation from invitations to engage in physical intimacy to safer topics centered around our children. I was hopeful those conversations would put his fire out because it seemed friendlier than directly smashing his heart with one more "I don't want to."

For years, these defensive tactics seemed relatively benign. I didn't think twice about skimping by with occasional time together. My marriage seemed great, and we were happy. I followed the advice given by the monsters in my head—to keep things cool and sleep-oriented—but I struggled because, although my marriage was fine, I also knew it was bland. Deep within, I wanted romance and a connection with my spouse rivaling all love stories ever told. I concluded we didn't have that because I was too afraid to show up as an equal in my marriage. I knew something had to change, because it was not sustainable (nor was it the goal) to remain periodically celibate. Instead of trying to find fault in my husband, I examined my own issues with intimacy.

I began to imagine what could happen if I continued to employ passive and evasive maneuvers in the bedroom. *A chasm divides us, my husband on one side and me on the other. I've been expecting him to come to rescue me the way he's always done. But as I imagine myself on one side of a canyon, I realize he can't always traverse that canyon. Expecting him to always come to me is not realistic. I am capable of meeting him halfway. Why haven't I moved toward him?*

I needed to embrace vulnerability rather than run from it. I needed to expand my vision for care and mutuality within our relationship. I needed to discover God's heart for husband and wife and learn sex is not about duty, but it's an invitation to deeply enjoy and satisfy one another. I wasn't going to achieve a deep caliber of connection by playing defense and shutting down romantic advances.

One afternoon it hit me: my sex life was not what I had envisioned for myself.

*What? I have an ideal sex life?*

This realization floored me. Winning is only possible if I get in the game. I was done with fear dictating my beliefs about love. I started claiming the truth about my relationship with my husband, and with every true statement, I clawed my way to the surface of worthiness.

I am MARRIED to the man I have been entranced by for nearly 17 years.

My husband is the man who blew all the other men out of the water and won my heart.

He is my soulmate and I am his.

He has never once made me feel unworthy of his love.

Every time I have been courageous enough to be vulnerable with him, he has accepted me with love and tenderness.

To write the love story I wanted, I had to step out of the shadows and change the narrative. I learned to play offense instead of defense. As soon as I recognized things needed to change, I made myself some promises to build a romantic relationship that would satisfy me, delight him, and benefit us both.

I've challenged myself to embody confidence, act instead of think, and communicate clearly.

As I continue to do these things, our love deepens and we grow closer as a couple. I have come to enjoy my physical relationship with my husband more than I ever thought possible. We have a stronger connection because we trust each other with the most tender places of our souls. I have more confidence in myself because I shame my body less. I have realized sex is a part of my humanity, and I participate in it with my dearly loved husband without guilt or shame. The love I have in my heart is not meant to be saved for a rainy day. It is meant to be given generously to my husband, knowing he will deeply nourish me as he meets me in that generosity.

Life is too damn short, ladies, not to invest in the most fulfilling intimate relationship you can create with the man you've married. We are all going to blink one day and years will have passed us by. We can't afford to be complacent in our lifelong relationships. We are meant to flourish, with deep roots and wide branches. Don't wait for the planets to align or until everything is perfect to tend your intimacy.

You have permission to cultivate a mutually satisfying romance with your spouse—one in which you take the bull by the horns, choosing action over passivity. Step out of your comfort zone and be courageous. Forge a rock-solid connection with your man. Stop playing defense, shooting down every arrow, and start taking your own shots with Cupid's bow. Focus your wild passion on that man lying next to you, and see if the unbridled love you give isn't returned to you tenfold.

Heart: See him over there in the office typing away on his computer?

Me: Yeah, he's pretty cute.

Heart: You want to surprise him?

Me: Of course! That sounds like fun.

Heart: Go get him, Tiger. He'll never know what hit him.

I walk up quietly behind him and lightly trace his shoulder and lean in to whisper in his ear.

"I think you're sexy."

His face melts into a smile. He knows I see him. I want him more now than when we first stoked the sparks between us.

# FANTASTIC

*Melissa Hogarty*

"Mommy, you look fantastic," my daughter declares when she rounds the bend and catches sight of me standing next to the kitchen table. *Fantastic* is her word of the week. She has been practicing it for days, and I can tell she is impressed with herself every time she spits out all three syllables in the right order.

I am dressed to go on a date with my husband. I've put on makeup, adding contours to my round face that simply don't exist without cosmetic assistance. I am wearing a long, flowered maxi-dress that bulges out over my pregnant belly, and I pinned my long braid into a knot at the nape of my neck.

For the first time in days, I feel attractive.

Miraculously, this date night thing has become a week-ly gig—we hired a college student home on her summer vacation to watch our kids every Thursday night. At first, our dates were romantic, rekindling the dreams we had when we were just dating. We explored new games at a board game café. We went to an open mic night and whispered about what songs we would play if we were on stage.

But then...our dates turned into errands. Last week, we spent our "date night" buying a suit for Dave so he could be a groomsman at a childhood friend's wedding.

And tonight, we are headed to the rehearsal dinner.

Lately, it seems like these evenings together are not a chance to reclaim who we were as husband and wife before we had two kids (and a third on the way), but a chance to tie up loose ends or arrange someone else's big day. I can't help but feel a pang of jealousy when I think about the bride-to-be, a young and carefree woman who smiles easily and honestly...and probably doesn't spend an hour attempting to give her face discernible cheekbones.

I bend down and give my 3-year-old a hug. "Thank you!" I whisper into her hair. She wraps her arms around my shoulders and squeezes.

She intended to compliment me, but my daughter has no idea how much I needed to hear her encouragement. I know I will feel out of place at the rehearsal dinner, the only pregnant wife among a crowd of strangers sipping champagne. I desperately want to look beautiful.

Beautiful is my shield against feeling awkward.

Sometimes I feel like my dial got stuck on "high school dance." If I do my nails and wear something flowy, no one will realize that underneath the shine is a girl who is terrified of making a wrong move and embarrassing herself.


After dinner, the groom hustles over to us. I am flushed and a little sweaty for no obvious reason. *Thanks, Baby,* I inwardly groan. The groom holds out his arms exuberantly, and I cautiously offer him a side hug, careful not to lift my arm too high in case the sweat has also created a smell.

"Melissa! I was just telling Dave at the rehearsal—" here, my husband bows with a flourish—"we are going to have live music for our first dance! And I convinced him to play the keyboard!"

I smile and nod. "That's perfect. I wouldn't expect anything less at your wedding!" This is the friend who keeps a spare guitar in his car, just in case he ever thinks of a song. At our wedding, he spontaneously serenaded the guests in the church lobby while we posed for family photos.

"Hey!" the groom goes on, as if something has just occurred to him. "You should play, too! Bring your guitar! The more the merrier."

I laugh and gesture down at my enormous belly. I can feel anxiety rising.

I enjoy singing in front of people, but I do *not* enjoy playing the guitar when strangers might hear me. And without my beautiful shield (because, let's face it, I am not feeling so pretty in this somewhat moist moment), there is little chance I can escape with my pride. Someone is bound to take a picture of the impromptu band, and there I will be, a hundred weeks pregnant, attempting to contort my unwieldy body to both hold *and strum* a guitar, while not showing an ounce of desperation or exertion on my face.

Plus, the wedding is two days away, and I've never even heard the song before. This is a recipe for disaster.

Unfortunately, it's hard to say no to an eager groom right before his wedding. So I say yes.

*Pep talk time.*

*No one is going to pay any attention to you, Melissa. You will be the background noise.*

I pry a bobby pin open with my teeth and shove it into the back of my hair, anchoring the long, straight strands safely away from my face.

I step back from the mirror and study myself. Nothing in my teeth. Not yet obviously struggling with the contacts I decided to put in an hour ago. *This will have to do.*

Suddenly, I remember the first time my husband and I prayed together, just after we started dating. He was sitting on the floor in the room I rented, telling me about a tough situation with a friend. I sat down next to him, and we bowed our heads to pray for healing. When we were through, he looked at me with an expression I can only describe as awe and said, "*Tu alma bonita.*" Your beautiful soul. (To clarify: neither of us is actually a Spanish speaker, but he was trying to impress me. And he did.)

What attracted him to me was not my lip gloss or my sense of style. It certainly wasn't my obsession with my body shape and size—something we both wish I didn't wrestle with to this day. It was my soul.

I examine my reflection in the mirror again. There I am. Brown hair and brown eyes. Lacy navy dress I love— maybe more than any other dress I've ever worn, maternity or otherwise. Currently serving as home to a second human.

Why do I struggle so hard to find pregnancy beautiful when I am the one wearing it?

Why is it so hard to see the beautiful soul underneath the mascara?

*Pep talk. Take two.*

*You are beautiful—yes, you—but this day is not about you, remember?*

*I know you are worried about being awkward, but your pride isn't the point. All eyes will be on the bride. It doesn't matter if you look fantastic or look like you need a fan. It doesn't matter if you hold your guitar at a strange angle or play the wrong chord. Just go play your best, because your friend asked you to. In the end, he will remember you showed up.*

When my daughter barely waves goodbye, offering no words of affirmation about my dress or my sparkly necklace, I don't ask. I don't want her to think the outside is anything more than a decoration.

I smile to myself and give a quick nod. Time to go.

# BLOOD, SWEAT, AND TEARS

*Emily Sue Allen*

MID-AFTERNOON SUN STREAMED THROUGH THE brown linen curtains, blanketing the room in a soft, warm glow. I'd left my oldest there on my bed with some books for a quiet reading time while her brothers slept in the next room, and I returned to find her asleep under her heavy, pink horse blanket with her books discarded to the other side of the bed. With our days-old new baby wrapped in a pink polka-dot swaddle, cheek pressed against my shoulder, I marveled to myself about all four kids being somehow asleep at the same time. A miracle, I tell you!

We had the perfect family. Two boys, two girls. Apparently all willing to nap collectively at the same time to give their weary mom an afternoon breather. Grace. It was a beautiful moment in time, the mess of birth behind me and what I thought would be my last ride through the ragged early years.

She was a March baby, and for months after her arrival, my husband and I generally agreed our family was complete.

He pounced on opportunities to announce to multiple people we knew, sometimes awkwardly, "No more babies." We were done. I was at peace with the decision, but in the quiet of my heart, I was not all-the-way, *absolutely* sure.

I was, however, beginning to dream about life after pregnancy, picking up the pieces of my done-in-the-cracks-of-time photography business. Entering the professional photography arena a few years prior had been a financial lifeline for our family—and personally it turned out to be a fulfilling creative outlet. I edited photos in the hours after our kids had gone to bed and photographed weddings or family photo sessions on the weekend when my husband wasn't at work.

Over the years, I'd shot a handful of births for friends, and the beauty of it gripped me. A child's entrance to the world is nothing short of a miracle, every time, and capturing the details of the event is a great honor. With my growing brood of children at home, I had given up on my desire to shoot births professionally because I couldn't figure out the logistics of being on call for them without more robust childcare options than we had then. But as the year wore on and my newborn daughter sprouted into a lively, playful, sitting baby, I felt the itch to look into it again, hoping some internet research would yield the secrets about how other people made it happen while they had children at home.

I typed a few terms into the search bar, and websites for birth photographers quickly populated the screen. I hoped to scan their information and policies to glean insight into how they remain available for on call assignments. Instead, I found myself sucked into slideshow after slideshow of women in various stages of labor. The anticipation. Intensifying contractions. Leaning on support. Retreating into a private internal place to focus through pain. I found myself holding my breath with each passing image, anticipating the baby's arrival. Tears started knocking at the back of my eyes as the moment of delivery drew near, and the swell of love, relief, wonder, and the sacred sight of a brand new life in the mother's arms broke open the dam. Hunched over my computer, clicking through images of women I didn't even know, I was sobbing ugly sobs, remembering my own birth experiences and lamenting what I thought to be the close of my childbearing season. I had been at peace with leaving behind the exhaustion and uncertainty of pregnancy and postpartum recovery, but as I witnessed birth slideshows, the beauty of bringing new life into the world (and the reality I would not do that again myself) was heavy.

A gentle voice whispered to my soul, "Emily, you are free to close this door if you want to, but if you're open to what I have for you, I'd love for you to trust me in your reproductive choices going forward." It was so gentle. So unexpected. And I decided at that moment that yes, I would trust the Lord for whatever He had for me.

I was nervous to share this idea with my husband, thinking he would shut down the idea immediately, but as I blubbered out my new desires to remain open, he simply said, "I know. I'm on board with that."

A year later, I sat at our dining room table with my family over takeout, very round with our fifth child, a girl. I'd been on baby watch for weeks, paying close attention to every tiny symptom that could be signaling labor. I have a history of intense, short labors—the longest of my previous four deliveries was a full three and a half hours; the shortest was two centimeters to ten in 45 minutes.

I birthed my first four children each at different hospitals, but after those four mad dashes to the delivery room—arriving with little time to spare—I planned for a home birth the fifth time around. It would be comforting to have a midwife come to me instead of sweating bullets about potentially having a baby in the car.

I was waddling everywhere I went, eager to be done with that part of pregnancy. A week prior, I had a false alarm and called the midwife over to my house, only to see my contractions dissipate over the course of an hour. My discomfort and disappointment were at an all-time high, and I started feeling more than a little desperate to get this little lady out.

I left the dinner table early, while the kids were still eating, because I was extremely tired. I went to my room, closed the door and the curtains, and laid my big whale belly on the bed.

I had shut my eyes for half an hour when it happened. With a sudden, weird-feeling pop, my water broke, and I zipped out of bed knowing this was going to be a fast and furious ride.

The contractions were offensive within the first ten minutes, and my midwife was the first call.

By the time she got to my house fifteen minutes later, I was quarantined in my bathroom, rocking back and forth on the toilet through contractions every third minute.

I closed my eyes and breathed forcefully to get through the pain.

*Open and out*, I thought to myself. I tried to relax more than I braced, but the height of every contraction made my shoulders tense up to my ears.

I wanted the baby out, but I was scared. I knew too

much about the physics of this operation. The work ahead both terrified me and also could not come soon enough.

I was ready and not ready. I knew I was strong, but I also felt fragile—tender and aware that giving birth is the messy meeting of heaven and humanity.

The midwife put the doppler on my belly to hear the little one's heart rate every so often, and I had to restrain myself from waving it away in the midst of my swaying and rocking in rhythm. I was deeply focused on overcoming each excruciating contraction, which continued to come with vigor.

At every peak, I wanted to crumble. I dug around for the grit in my bones to press forward, to open and surrender instead of bracing against the pain. Between the swells, I momentarily felt like I could do it. In the clutches of another contraction, I sank low, tensed up my shoulders, and hoped that someday the agony would end.

*Help. Help. Help.*

These were my one-word prayers, sputtered out through intense pain, fear of what was coming, and the distress of waiting to be delivered of this child over the course of ninety minutes.

It all started to feel impossible, like the pain would never end. The baby would never come out and I would never open my eyes again. I could not remember what not-pain felt like.

My husband and the midwife each grabbed an arm and hobbled me from the toilet to the twin mattress prepared on the floor just outside the bathroom door—a makeshift maternity ward close to running water. I heard myself scream and felt contortions of my body I could not control, my eyes still tightly closed. I knew nothing except the strong arms that kept me from breaking apart—the arms of my husband who held me through the last frightful minutes. I was terrified. I was screaming. I was frozen.

And then she was there. My heart and womb spilled out; a perfect miracle of a baby girl wailing on my bare chest. Together, we were the bloodiest, sweatiest, most beautiful sight.

I cried from pain, relief, and wonder.

*My beautiful child.*

Motherhood, like birth, is a messy, raw, and visceral experience—but it is also profoundly beautiful.

Through desperate breath prayers and writhing pain, mothers bring new life to the earth.

With sweat and blood and fierce mama love, we conquer fears and discover our strength again and again.

Through tears and uncertainty, we give life from our own bodies and nurture our children to maturity at great personal cost.

When we embrace the sacrifices required to compassionately guide our children through their developmental years, we grow alongside them in love, in character, and in beauty.

This is why I cry every time I see a newborn baby in a mother's arms. This is why I will spend my life reminding mothers: motherhood will cost you blood, sweat, and tears, but your investment into your children's lives is a worthy, important, and meaningful way to spend yourself.

In this spending, in this spilling out, you, mama, are profoundly, wondrously beautiful.

# PART V

# STRONG AND BRAVE

*Lindsey Cornett*

L ONG BEFORE I KEPT A BOX OF PREGNANCY TESTS IN MY medicine cabinet, I created a Pinterest board labeled "Baby Nursery Ideas." When my daughter was born—our third child but the first girl—we were just about to move into a new house. Her room needed the most work: new floors, a new door, repaired baseboards, and many coats of paint. Oh, the Pinterest browsing I did! I wanted the room to be feminine but not in a traditional sense. I wanted it to be modern but not too trendy—no stereotypes. And, of course, I hoped the nursery would somehow convey all my hopes and dreams for her life. No pressure, right? Wrong. So much pressure. So much internet-inspired, perfectionist pressure.

Ruthie lived her first two years in that room. It was not quite magazine-worthy, but it was cute and cozy. A watercolor painting by my grandmother—Ruthie's namesake— hung on the wall, next to a basket of books and headbands.

To the right of the bedroom door, I hung some typography art from a big box store. (You know the kind: perpetually 40% off, very on-trend, meant to appear hand-painted but totally isn't.) Nestled within a geometric pattern were three simple words: "strong and brave." Every time Ruthie woke from a nap or I finished folding pink onesies into her drawers, I turned toward the door to leave her room, and I saw it: strong and brave.

"Words of affirmation" has never been my love language. When I was 5 or 6 years old, my parents signed me up for golf lessons. Once a week, my dad and I drove to a local country club, where an elderly security guard waited at the gate to grant us permission to enter. Each time we pulled up to the guard stand, my dad rolled down his window, pointed to me, and said, "This is a Future LPGA champ, right here!" I was mortified. I began making up excuses to get out of my lessons: too much homework, a headache, too sleepy. Eventually, my parents figured out I didn't want to go to golf lessons, but I never told them why. I just couldn't stand that moment of cheesy, braggadocious, but perfectly sweet enthusiasm from my dad. Affirmations have always made me feel a little squirmy.

I've never felt particularly strong or brave, even before having children. I avoid scary movies (and even their trailers) lest I have nightmares for a week. I don't play sports or work out. I cry easily and am hypersensitive. In college, I introduced myself to a neighbor solely because I needed him to come kill a spider in my apartment. (I wish I was joking.) Throughout the years, I allowed my own insecurities and cultural messages to convince me I was both weak and cowardly.

At first blush, my daily life, to-do list, and calendar

don't do much to inspire images of bravery or strength. I wipe a lot of snotty noses, sweep up a lot of Cheerios, and send a lot of GIFs in text messages to my husband. I read stories about my personal heroes, and they are brave in ways I can barely imagine. I think of the fortitude required of a mother who has buried a child, a wife whose husband has left, a father working two jobs, children who walk to school in war-torn, violent cities. I'm a white, middle class, Christian woman with a husband at home—I'm aware there are women whose lives require more strength and bravery than my own.

Still, this doesn't at all diminish the strength and courage I've cultivated in my lived story. I carried and birthed three children in less than four years. I moved 1,200 miles across the country, away from all my family and friends. I reimagined my career and vocation several times. I show up for church most Sundays. I make an effort to listen to the voices of people who are different from me. I have met with senators and handed out pamphlets to talk about issues of significance. Once upon a time, I taught a class of 18 first-graders in a public school. I've submitted essays to websites and been rejected and still tried again. I asked for help when postpartum depression seemed to be getting the better of me.

When Ruthie was just a newborn, I turned to leave her room and the sign caught my eye differently than it ever had before. In a moment of quiet soul-realization, I knew it. I pulled my shoulders back, took a deep breath, and stood a little taller. *Strong and brave.*

Calling to mind my own spirit, I joyfully take my place among the strong and brave mothers who have gone before and walk beside me now. We are mothers with babies at our breasts and toddlers at our sides, with teenagers backing our SUVs down our driveways. We are mothers on the sidelines of football games and in the lobbies of infertility clinics. We are mothers at social workers' offices or in corporate cubicles. We are mothers with anti-anxiety prescriptions and mothers with gym memberships. Strength and courage are simply what motherhood requires of us.

Unwittingly, I had hung on Ruthie's wall the reminder I needed for myself all along. When we eventually moved to a new house and decided all three children would share a room, that "Strong and Brave" canvas was the first thing I hung on the wall.

Ruthie is 3 now, and at least once a day she proclaims, "Well, you know Mom, I am berry bwave." In Ruthie's world, smooshing a spider and walking into a dark room are both cause for affirmation: strong and brave, indeed. Within a few years, she will be old enough to read the inscription on that painting, but she may not even notice it. It will have been the backdrop of her entire life and, for her, may just blend right into the wall. So I will have to remind her. I'll point to it and say, "Strong and brave, Ruthie-love. That's you."

Like mother, like daughter.

# THIS BELLY

*Jacelya Jones*

T HIS BELLY, man. It's permanently inflated, I guess. The pronounced roundness of my belly ensures well-meaning women are regularly asking some variation of "How far along are you?" They find it hard to accept my "I'm not pregnant."

At forty, knowing another child would stretch my belly out again, I still wanted to get pregnant. So this fourth baby, even with her unpredictable arrival, was the sweetest reply to prayer I've ever received.

I started feeling nauseous at the smell of maple in the sausage I'd been making every day. I started wrinkling my nose as I perceived things no one else in our home detected. I started taking naps. The changes made Hubby and I decide at about the same time: better get a test. Then I barely peed on the stick, and it said, *strap in! She's coming!*

After a few prenatal checkups, I realized this was going

to be a different ride than my previous three pregnancies. I was labeled "at risk" because of my age. Then my blood pressure decided to spike. The doctors wanted to give me beta blockers. I'd been treated with those before, resulting in blood pressure so low I could barely move or speak or open my eyes. So I found a doctor who took me by the hand and asked how I thought we should walk as partners in my birth journey.

We agreed on what I felt was a safe treatment for the hypertension I was experiencing, but at the very end of my pregnancy, the numbers demanded delivery. We scheduled induction for the day before her due date. Instead, two things led to an emergency C-section the morning of her actual due date: I wasn't responding to the induction stimulants, yet Baby's heart rate was decreasing in response to them.

The nurses were so concerned that their fear spilled over as they talked in voices just loud enough for me to make out the words. Dread was etched into their faces, a glaze on their eyes as they checked the monitors.

"Is my baby going to die?" I asked. My heart felt big enough to explode with a worry I'd never experienced before. Too much of my mind was focused on how it was not supposed to be this way. *Why am I vomiting? Why haven't they sorted my anesthesia yet? Why is there a plastic drape down there? I won't see her when she comes out.*

My husband was allowed to come into surgery with me because I'd already received an epidural injection. (Thank God.) The Lord used him to anchor me after I was wheeled into the operating room. During surgery, they didn't cut her from my "belly," technically.

"The incision will be beneath your belly button," my OB and impromptu surgeon assured me as he stood smiling with another grinning stranger. It would be a slice into flesh—pulling muscles apart to reach the uterus—that wouldn't show in my bikini. In my twenty-something bikini days, I didn't appreciate my then-faultless figure as we climbed waterfalls and drank mocktails on the beach. I don't wear bikinis anymore and haven't since Jamaica with Hubby. They're in my past, and I'm fine with that. I don't miss them.

The scene in front of me before I ever saw her was beautiful. Impossibly so. I was able to discern the softening of my husband's face as, covered head to toe in a blue cap, mask, and scrubs, he took her from the doctors. His eyes were full of wonder, and looking at him, I knew without seeing for myself how amazing she would be.

Then Hubby brought her down to my face. I don't remember her tears. I don't even think she cried as she left behind life as she'd known it to join us in this one. I just remember her eyes. I imagined them being filled with heaven and its mysteries. I also saw recognition and love there. She opened her eyes so wide, trying to take in all of her mama. That look shook me like an earthquake. I could have understood and been more prepared if I had spoken and my voice had meant something to her. But I could not understand or anticipate that my face would mean something—that it would be known to her somehow.

When I shook Doc's hand between both of mine (the nearest I could come to the bear hug and kisses on both cheeks I wanted to give him) tears filled his wise eyes. My OB was sure he'd let me down because we had to shift the plan we'd so carefully made. His eyes and words anchored me. His heart for my dream, as well as the resources he brought and organized around it, were beautiful.

The first letter to the Thessalonians says: "Give thanks in all circumstances; for this is the will of God in Christ Jesus for you" (5:18). It isn't that I have to be thankful *for* all circumstances—incisions, injections, and scars—but *within* them, as I go through the graphic, yet beautiful, path to life.


Coming home, my belly had a lot of adjusting to do. She had to be disinfected with cotton swabs each day. Thankfully, Hubby was completely at ease, stepping in to help me with this because I still couldn't see my toes, let alone the crevice below the curve of my belly, just above my pubic bone. The former baby of the family couldn't climb into my lap and nestle against my belly or rest her curly head there anymore. My belly missed the warmth of her presence as my heart grieved the change, the quiet ending of our third child's reign as "the baby."

Our "Little Piggy," as we call her, changed everything about our home and family. She brought a tidal wave of love crashing over and into us. Almost 2 years old now, she is the first and only baby ever to gather reading books as a morning and nightly ritual. In the morning, her bed head spirals around in different directions as she heads to her changing table. It was handed down to us from beloved neighbor friends and subsequently turned into a keeping place for creams, oils, diapers, wipes, and woven baskets for clothing, toys, and books.

In the morning as I make the bed and also at night when we come up for bedtime, she heads to that cedar table for all her books, making rounds until she's piled them all together on our tall bed. Then, not looking for help, she heads to the foot of the bed, where there is a ledge for her tiny knees and feet. Gathering bedding in her nearly 2-year-old fists, she climbs up to her treasure. She pulls them around her and into her lap, humming one of her favorite songs—either "Yummy" by the Biebs or "The Goodbye Song" from her favorite show on the Yippee network, *Pete & Penelope*. "Daddy read!" she will demand in her sweet, mushy dialect. Or, if he's off somewhere and I'm brushing my teeth or something, she'll "read" to herself. It's wonderful.

My belly? She still refuses to be manipulated by the threadbare puppet strings of my abdominal muscles when I try to suck her in. And there isn't a cream that can handle the wild, raised marks running drunkenly, like mascara, over her face. But I don't flinch when the big kids touch her, or when the baby blows raspberries into her warm roundness. I'm not embarrassed by the way my clothes outline her curve anymore.

"I love my belly no matter what," I tell my 8-year-old as she stares up at me with her incredible, wide, brave eyes and fire-kissed dark curls. My top has blown up, exposing my belly, and she is trying to tuck me back in as the baby mashes her face into me happily. "I wouldn't have *you* without this belly," I say, smoothing back her sweet loops of deep reddish brown, bending at the waist to rub the baby's back.

# LIFELINE

*Lynne Patti*

I AM IN TEARS. Another failed attempt at homeschooling my 5-year-old daughter is now seared into the headspace I've entitled "Homeschool Scenarios Where I Fail." She's in tears too. Of course she's in tears. I've yelled at her for writing the letter "m" incorrectly and yelled again for blatantly refusing to practice reading a few silly words. I have nothing left. I'm holding my youngest baby, cooing and clueless, while my 2-year-old is passed out on the couch, probably exhausted from witnessing the debacle that is me trying to teach kindergarten to my eldest at home.

I am lonely. I feel unsupported. I am on an island, and the isolation and desolation are palpable. I need a lifeline—something to get me through.

I remember teaching my kids about the sinking of the Titanic, and like any good teenager of the '90s, I quickly recall the scene in *Titanic* when Rose comments on the number of lifeboats compared to the number of passengers, foreshadowing the clamoring and chaos that comes when the big boat is sinking. Motherhood is the same. Why do we so easily allow ourselves to embark on this epic journey without a plan for when days go awry and the icy water is about to engulf us?

I wipe my own tears and gently prod the 2-year-old to consciousness. I drag my body to the kitchen to piece together lunch. I feel like I'm groping for balance. For air. For connection.

I text our babysitter. "5:30 tonight? Still work?"

I wait for the lifeline.

My self-employed husband works in a studio off our garage, but he's not accessible between 9:00 and 5:00 because *boundaries.* He is 20 yards from me (the huddled, crying mess at the dining room table), yet he might as well be halfway across the Atlantic. I can't lean on him like I used to. A third baby and a mortgage means I get less of him than two years ago when it was just two babies in a rental.

Tonight, I want him 20 inches from me. I want someone to share in the ups and downs of this thing called parenting and help carry the load. I want us to abandon our phones and let time run away as we get lost in each other's words. I want a lifeline.

Then there's the guilt. I blew it with my daughter during school and now I'm abandoning her to a babysitter and running from the aftermath.

A spritely text lights up my phone: "Yup! I'll see you then!"

A lifeline. Help is on the way.


Mike and I get into the car and, after he turns off NPR, I let the quiet wash over me. No crying, no tugging, no yelling. One minute of silence. Ten breaths, uninterrupted.

I close my eyes. The day is already melting away into the background, and we've only just pulled out of the driveway.

"Okay, so I need your opinion on the music I wrote today," he says as we leave the neighborhood. I plug his phone into the audio port in the car, and we listen together to the track he's been working on. Our shared love of music and his trust in my opinion as a musician bond us together instantly.

We begin with some small talk, but we get to the heart of things quickly. He's struggling with the pressure of the multiple companies he runs, the employee dynamics, and the piling responsibilities. He reaches for my hand, and I pause to wonder about *his* lifelines. Does he ever hang on for dear life amid the chaos? What does he reach for? How does he find space to breathe?

I gently squeeze his hand and say, "Well, I put on make-up! Just for you." He smiles and says thank you, and we are off into the night, just him and me. No responsibilities for this one evening.

Each date night is different. Sometimes we explore restaurants or go for walks. We usually avoid the movies because we both prefer to be face-to-face, talking. Now and again, we sneak back to his work studio, separate from our house, and order takeout with explicit delivery instructions. ("Do NOT ring the doorbell. Come around back.") We enjoy our take-out Thai food while we sit in his little studio and catch up on *Vice News* or *The World's Most Extraordinary Homes*. We've had date nights at Costco (we needed a shed) or Target (we needed light bulbs). Mundane errands are made infinitely better when you're hanging out with your best friend.

Still, date nights are not always blissful and romantic. Some are hard. One night, just after we bought our first home, we sat in the car in a parking garage for several hours, and I listened as he struggled to navigate hard personal losses. His head in my lap, I was filled with empathy and compassion for him, yet I had to confess I was out of wifely solutions.

"I think you need to talk to someone else about this," I said, tentatively. "Maybe even get a counselor." We prayed. We cried. Not one baby or toddler near us needed a diaper change. No sassy, 5-year-old little girl lurked about. Only us. Husband and wife. Best friends. Discovering each other. Rediscovering each other. Date night conversations are not always sexy, but sometimes the conversations themselves become the lifeline.

We talk about family dynamics and politics. We laugh about our kids. We discuss God, mankind, and the problem of evil. We go through our memories like a slideshow, pausing to remember the whys and hows of each tableau. We marvel at the speed of the years. When we can get to this space—this quiet, uninterrupted, focused space—we are woven more tightly together: stronger, more unbreakable.

On this particular evening after the homeschool debacle, I let him unload work stuff, and he lets me process teaching our strong-willed child. "She'll be just fine. Say you're sorry tomorrow before you start school." Just like that, the burden lifts.

It's expensive. It's a lot of work. It's hard to find a good babysitter. Some days, it's hard to put on actual clothes and throw on eyeliner. It's hard to pump milk for a bottle. We've added babies and a new house and several new sitters to the team. The hardships have melted away into deeper love, deeper respect, and deeper intimacy. We've been investing in our marriage through weekly date nights for ten years now, and it has been worth every painstaking effort taken to get here.

The hours pass quickly. When we get home, the house is still, and the kitchen and living room all cleaned up. We exchange some brief small talk with our sitter, pay her, and she leaves. Intimacy through good conversation and good food leads to intimacy elsewhere. There's nothing left to be done downstairs, so we turn out the lights and kiss the children's sleeping heads. Then we reach for each other with no distractions, each of us a lifeline for the other.

We are one.

We.

He and I.

My forever boyfriend.

My kids' daddy.

My lover.

My best friend.

My lifeline.

# PAINT-SPECKLED MOTHER

*Robin Chapman*

I HAVE TO DO SOMETHING WITH THIS KITCHEN. I have lived with it for ten years. The dark brown cabinets with antique brass pulls and big decorative medallions beneath them. The bright orange countertops. The cracking linoleum—a mosaic of browns, oranges, and something like yellow, all shades resembling the inside of newborn diapers. In some seasons, I cease to notice, but today, I've decided I cannot live with it for one more second.

*This kitchen is older than my parents' marriage.*

Additionally, my children are being noisy and demanding. *How many pickles do y'all need in an afternoon?* The obvious answer to my building frustration with both the children and the kitchen: half an hour on Pinterest and one poorly planned, split-second decision. "Pack it up, kids, we're going to Lowe's."

I spend 15 seconds choosing a shade of gray to paint the cabinets. "Morning Fog" seems like a solid choice for a kitchen. Then I spend about five seconds more making yet another brilliant choice: "Big girls, if you can agree on a color, I will let you choose the paint for the interior of the lower cabinets." I leave them to make a choice while I take the preschoolers to customer service in search of someone who can mix paint. I return to find Jenna (8) on her hands and knees with Katherine (7) standing on her back to pick out the perfect shade from the top row of paint swatches: "Robust Pink." *Cool. Pepto Bismol with a hint of salmon seems appropriate for cabinetry.*

Thus began my first ever DIY home project.

Over the following several weeks, I learned some important lessons. For instance, always take off the bottom hinge before the top when removing cabinet doors, otherwise you must catch the door before you get whacked in the noggin. (Hypothetically.) Always use primer unless you want to paint four coats of Robust Pink before coverage is almost sufficient. Also, 45 years of kitchen grease will not be handled by sanding. (Ick.) Wear a hat when you paint the inside of cabinets. Related: just because you wash your hair (and rinse and repeat!), don't assume the paint flecks will be gone. The parts of your arms likeliest to be paint-smeared are also the parts you are least likely to notice and scrub. You will look ridiculous in public for the duration of this project.

I plugged along, starting with the lower interiors and the slightly-coral bright pink. I painted and painted and painted again. I bought a can of high-coverage Kilz to prime the next portion of espressoish brown. (I say "ish" because espresso is a great color. This…was not.) Then I was on to drawers, sticking down contact paper, and refilling the bottom cabinets to make space in my dining room for the contents of the uppers. When it came to the orange counters (neon pumpkin?), I enlisted the help of a friend with a fine arts degree—my own BS in math was zero help to me here. I removed caulk, scrubbed, patched, and primed the Formica. She directed the work of making them look like granite. Up next came the cabinet doors that had taken over the space where we usually eat dinner.

It took a couple months to decide what to do with the floors—the linoleum was horrifying, but we planned to eventually refloor the living room and dining room together (the dining room is carpeted, which is possibly the worst, as are the living room, hallway, and bedrooms), and I wasn't ready to refloor the whole main level just yet. So I caulked the holes in the floor and painted it. I bought deck paint, thinking, *it's made for foot traffic! Should be perfect.* I painted the floor white, then laid down masking tape "grout lines" and put a coat of dark gray over that. Lessons learned: this is a poor project to tackle during winter. When the temperature outside is sub-zero and you can't get any ventilation, painting with materials *clearly* meant for outdoor use will make you unintentionally high. (Oops.) All the same, the janky floor update was, in fact, an improvement, even if the lines weren't straight, and random *very* long hairs got sealed under the polyurethane.

Why did I decide to take on my entire kitchen based on one crappy-in-the-usual-way afternoon and 20 seconds' deliberation after living with a kitchen straight out of the '70s for ten years? I still cannot tell you.

I spent an entire month sanding, painting, and yelling at my children to stay out of the kitchen and *do not touch the wet paint! For the love!*

It ended up taking three full months to finish. In the weeks following, I realized the cabinet hinges weren't quite right—their screws stripped out, which means my kitchen is currently missing a couple of cabinet doors. So even though it's finally "done," it's not *done*. It's fine.

The question I've asked might be the same one you're asking: do I regret this? Was it a bad choice to spend 20 seconds considering a project that would take more than a month to complete? Do I even like what it's becoming? No, I don't regret it. Given what it looked like before, pretty much *any* change is an improvement. (Also, Robust Pink is a great conversation starter.)

Those darn antique brass medallions under the door pulls had annoyed me for ten years, but I was having babies all that time. It was never a convenient time to consider improvement options, make decisions, spend money, disrupt the kitchen, and spend several weeks working to finish it. This is not a good time to do any of those things either. I doubt I would ever have stumbled upon a "good" time, but I do like what it's becoming. It's brighter, which is important in the middle of an Alaskan winter, with its four hours of daylight. It's cleaner—the light gray doesn't hide things like the dark brown did (again, ICK). And it's been good to have my children see me doing the project. I realized they hadn't seen me wield a drill before, much less a palm sander. (My husband is unusually handy, so outsourcing to him is always the expedient option.) I needed us all to remember I'm a capable human and allowed to make big changes too.

It turns out I have agency. I spend so much of my life responding to my kids and their situations. Recently, I read in a John Gottman book, "Behavioral psychologists have observed that preschoolers typically demand that their caretakers deal with some kind of need or desire at an average rate of three times a minute." Three times a minute. No wonder I live my whole life responding— or, more likely, reacting—to them. Four kids times three requests per minute means I am handling their needs or responding to requests (often "no" with subsequent sadness from them) every five seconds, on average. No hyperbole. Every. Five. Seconds. *Of course* I have a hard time making proactive decisions. With only five-second intervals available, I can barely even breathe. I needed to make a decision about my kitchen in a few seconds because a few seconds was *all I had.*

My children and I all need to remember that they can absolutely survive for a few weeks on PB&Js, Disney+, and vague instructions hollered from a paint-speckled mother inventing new and awkward yoga poses to prime the hard-to-reach areas. ("I call this one 'Drunken Emu.' It is for painting the bottom side of the cabinet above the fridge.") I don't have to be on call for requests, questions, and demands every five seconds. I'm a grown woman—I can make actual decisions that make my spaces more pleasant for me to live in, and I don't always need thoroughly researched answers before I start.

Sometimes a few seconds is all I need to make a decision: It's time to begin.

# JUST CAITLIN

*Melissa Hogarty*

O N THE WAY HOME FROM PRESCHOOL, my middle daughter usually keeps up a steady stream of inane chatter. She talks about the art projects she did that morning and conversations we had yesterday. I give myself permission to listen with only one ear, rotating through several noncommittal exclamations. "Really? Hm. That sounds interesting."

But this afternoon, as she gazes out the window toward the scruffy green pines lining the far side of the highway, she is quiet. I appreciate the relative silence of our drive, the ample room it provides for my wandering mind, until she suddenly announces, "I never want to be a mom."

I'm glad she can't see my face directly as I process this statement. *Never?* I struggle briefly with feeling judged, hurt that my life as a stay-at-home mom already feels like an inadequate aspiration to her. What does she see in me that makes her want the opposite?

"Why not?" I ask, searching for her face in the rearview

mirror. I keep my voice light and even, in the small, probably vain hope she will forget all about this if I don't make it a big deal. Like all preschoolers, she has a fickle way of disregarding things I'd like her to remember, but grabbing the horns of ideas I wish would run away.

"Because I want to be a ballerina. And a real artist!" she exclaims. In the edge of the mirror, I can see her wide, earnest eyes as she looks toward me.

"Oh," I say lamely. After a pause, "You know, mommies can do all kinds of things! You could be a dancer *and* a mommy if you want to."

"I know!" she replies gamely, tilting her head forward and raising her palms for emphasis. She pastes on her biggest squinty-eyed smile. "But..." she trails off for a moment. Then her voice takes on a squeaky cheerfulness, rising in pitch as if she is opening Door Number 3 to reveal my prize. "I just don't want to be a mom."

I want to tell her I found myself after becoming a mother. Not in that cheesy, motherhood-made-me-whole kind of way. No. Being a mother pushed me to the absolute end of myself. When I was hanging on by a thread, I started wondering what I wanted from my life. That was when I finally remembered my childhood dream of being a writer.

*Ta-daaa!* I want to shout. *I'm doing it! I'm doing now what I didn't have the courage to fail at before motherhood.*

I want to tell Caitlin about this recently rediscovered joy. I want to tell her being a mom won't stop her from doing the things she loves. Moms can be artists and coaches and entrepreneurs and engineers. If you want to make something amazing happen, ask a mom.

But I button my lips. I know trying to force this issue, trying to convince Caitlin that God may call her into motherhood or that motherhood is worthwhile will only make her dig in her heels.

I always hoped having a daughter would be like looking in a mirror. This hope was born of reading too many novels whose authors imagined too few original characters. Fictional daughters are so often the spitting image of their mothers, waving their hands in the same way, sharing similar habits and pet peeves, speaking in the same dulcet tones.

My life as an avid reader built me up to be shocked when I became the mother of girls.

My mirror turned out to be the one from *Mary Poppins*. While I calmly smooth my hair, thinking I see and hear echoes of myself, my daughter Caitlin is preparing for her glorious solo. She sings and dances when she wants to, and her choices have little to do with me. I am left staring through the glass in astonishment as a completely separate, cheeky person lives her own life in her own way.

I should probably be grateful she makes her own music and follows it. I once googled "strong-willed children" and learned that someday my daughter will be less likely to succumb to peer pressure. All her practice saying no to *me* may grow her into a young woman who can lead others confidently.

This doesn't help me right now.

At age 4, my "middlest daughter" takes pure joy in discovering the ways she is different from me. It started with bananas, which she would happily eat all day long, while I gag from the smell. It grew to encompass pictures of bugs and so much more. Sometimes, learning I like something will send her scuttling into the enemy camp merely for the fun of being contrary.

Yet she desperately wants the fellowship of being seen and known. She likes to tell me what she's thinking by assuming I already know. "You know I never want to go to Egypt because they have scorpions," or, "You know applesauce is my favorite snack, Mommy."

*Yes. I do know. You told me this yesterday. And the day before that.*

One day, I suppose, she may assume the opposite. She may assume I don't know anything about her—that I couldn't possibly understand. She just doesn't realize it's already true. I catch glimpses I recognize—her love of books, her goofy smiles, her interest in singing and dancing—but mostly, she is a mystery to me.

Why, for example, does she prefer to sleep on her floor instead of in her bed? Night after night, I tuck her in and say goodnight, only to find her scrunched on the floor an hour later, snoozing next to a line of books I swear we put away before bedtime.

Why does she reject adjectives? When she turned 3, Caitlin informed me that being called "little one" hurt her feelings. Within days, a parade of other adjectives met a stubborn end. Caitlin does not want to be called beautiful or brave or strong or creative or happy.

She isn't any of those things, she tells me.

She is just Caitlin.


I still carry around the unspoken adjectives in my heart with her silly, easy laughter and her confident belief in what she can do. I can see beauty, even as she shakes herself free from my interpretation of her.

It turns out, the advice I want to give her in the car is the same advice I need to hear myself: don't cling so tightly. Be open to how God may write the twists and turns in Caitlin's story.

It's certainly possible that one day, her (not little) heart-shaped face will resemble my oval one. She may turn out to share common interests with me. Maybe she will call herself a mother and homemaker.

Or maybe she will become a photographer for *National Geographic* and live the kind of itinerant life that would terrify me.

My job as her mom is not to walk her through the exact same joy I found. No matter what God calls her to, she will never become a mirror image of me—and I'm glad. I would much rather see her reflecting the image of Christ. My job is simply to point her face toward Jesus and hold her hand until she is ready to walk in joy of her own.

# SHADES OF PURPLE

*Bethany McMillon*

I PLOP DOWN ON THE COUCH WITH EVERY INTENTION OF searching for a new recipe to prepare for dinner. Instead, I switch apps and scroll through social media where I find evidence of one friend's family trip overseas, a romantic weekend away with a husband, and friends celebrating their 100th workout together. Within minutes, my spirit shifts from a peaceful, relaxing (albeit indecisive) evening with my son to feeling like I'm not quite enough.

I set my phone aside, inwardly roll my eyes at how quickly my mood has changed, and consider a pre-dinner walk. Suddenly irritated by every aspect of life, I know the walk will do me good. And maybe by the time I get back, I'll have an idea of what I can pull together for a family meal.

My son's head is bent over homework. His finger winds through his hair, twisting like he always does when he's deep in thought. The remnants of his after-school snack sit next to his books. My husband won't be home for at least another half hour. No one will starve before I return.

Out the door, I fall into a rhythm.

Step. Inhale. Step. Exhale. Step. Listen. Step. Notice.

Walking outside soothes my soul. When noise and feelings begin to overwhelm me, I leave the earbuds at home. I need a silent walk. The simplicity of one foot in front of the other reestablishes a steady pace for my mind. I take in the refreshing sounds of neighborhood chatter, the birds, and the breeze.

As my eyes adjust to the muted sunshine of evening, I notice the array of green around our neighborhood. I breathe out my disquieted spirit and whisper worship, in awe of God's artistry.

Slowly, God reveals His brilliance in new ways. My eyes shift. It isn't the green that captivates me now, it is purple flowers dotting the path.

With each turn, in each yard and vacant lot, I behold their beauty. My steps quicken and my eyes dart around to soak in all the stunning shades of purple: some buds are pale, barely purple; others lilac, royal purple, and electric.

The Spirit whispers, "Consider the lilies of the field, how they grow: they neither toil nor spin, yet I tell you, even Solomon in all his glory was not arrayed like one of these" (Matthew 6:28-29).

My spirit catches this truth. Our beauty is like purple flowers. At first glance, we are simply moms, plain purple blossoms along the walks of life.

But to our Creator, to our family, to those that love us, care for us, and treasure us, we are beautifully diverse shades. We are lilac, lavender, periwinkle, and amethyst. We are plum, boysenberry, and eggplant.

Our personalities, viewpoints, and experiences all shade

our lives, making us distinctly perfect for our place in our garden. My family simply needs me to be the person God is creating *me* to be.

My mind turns back to the social media images. Before my walk, it felt like each one convicted me as not enough. Now I can see the beauty in each of the moms, uniquely called to their families and their specific circumstances: moms gifted with a great sense of adventure, couples with a bent toward romance, and friends who bond over pushing each other to new limits.

We celebrate the story of pasts that color us a vibrant magenta or a lively violet. We rejoice in the personality traits that tint us pale iris or soft heather. We delight in the individual gifts that shade us deep plum or warm sangria.

With my new realization in mind, I turn home.

"Hey Mom, how was your walk?" my boy asks as he welcomes me in the door. We chat about the sunset and football stats and a new book being released in a series he's reading. I rummage through the pantry and refrigerator, still debating what to cook for dinner.

Soon, he stands beside me. "What about peanut butter and jelly sandwiches?" he suggests. "You make the best ones."

I laugh. Though he now looks me in the eye, his sandwich requirements have been identical since he was tiny—a smear of creamy peanut butter from crust to crust on both pieces of bread and a smattering of homemade strawberry jelly, no crust allowed.

We pull out the ingredients together and enjoy our simple dinner in relative quiet.

"Thanks, Mom. PB&Js are kind of your superpower," he says as he clears the table.

I make a killer PB&J. I am both steady and flexible. I listen well and cherish different perspectives. Each of these traits makes me the exact right shade of purple for our little family.

# PINBALL MOM

*Lynne Patti*

I SIT WITH MY 3-YEAR-OLD DAUGHTER IN THE DINING room as she kicks and screams. I've tried holding her, talking to her, and yelling at her, yet nothing is working to calm her.

"Why did Mommy put you in time-out?"

She bellows at me incoherently.

"Ellie, you stole the mints from the van. That's why I put you in time-out. Can you tell me that? Why did I put you in time-out?"

I'm asking her to repeat to me *why* (to bring closure and hopefully understanding through this disciplinary action), but I might as well be speaking Dutch because she is not tracking, and the tantrum rages on.

Rewind: she went missing just before lunch as I was finishing up homeschool with my older kids. We found her (quickly enough I didn't panic) in the garage. She had climbed into the front seat of my van (we keep the door open during the day sometimes), squirreling away LifeSaver mints into her pocket and her mouth as fast as she could. She got caught red-handed, so the whole time-out scene ensued.

I never love the disciplinary gauntlet my 3-year-old throws down for me. I know it's necessary, but it's exhausting.

Fast forward: she finally admits she stole the mints. Minutes after hugs and sorries—Daddy gets the littlest two settled for quiet time—I'm bopping along in the famous mint-laden van (minus a few) on my way to Costco with my 12-year-old daughter and 9-year-old son, harmonizing at the top of our lungs to *Hamilton* blasting over the car stereo. (Sometimes we do three-part harmony, and it's amazing.)

"Mom, what does *ironic* mean?" my son asks over the musical din. I search my brain's database and all I can come up with is Alanis Morissette circa 1995. (If you're past a certain age, it's now in *your* head—you're welcome.) I ask my daughter/copilot/DJ to leave "Angelica, Eliza, (and Peggy)" in favor of a hit single from decades ago. My son loves the song and comes up with his own irony: you buy all the toilet paper in Costco, and then don't use any of it (thank you very little, COVID-19).

As we wander the wide aisles of Costco, I point at things we need and my little-big shoppers load the things into the cart.

"Okay, grab the bread there...can you get the bag of chips? Oh, and put some ground turkey into one of those plastic bags. I don't want it to leak. Do you think we need croissants this week?"

"Mom—let's get muffins!!!"

"No," I say, decidedly. I know muffins from Costco are

really just cake. I can't quite justify cake for breakfast—at least not this week. Nor can I justify the muffin/cake crumbs that fill up the house every time we splurge and buy them.

"I have to go to the bathroom," my son whispers to me.

"No problem! You know where it is, at the front by the registers. Go on ahead and I'll meet you right by the walk-in cooler where the grapes and blueberries are. Got it?"

"Got it!" he yells with his back already toward me as he confidently runs to the front of the store. I pause and remember how, just a few blinks ago, both of these kids had their legs dangling from the front of a double Costco cart. Sending one off to the bathroom by himself was, in my mind, akin to sending him off to college. But not anymore. Now, not only can he walk by himself, but he can also navigate his way through this massive store, use the restroom by himself, and then return to me.

I shake myself out of this reverie as I see him come bounding back to me by the produce walk-in, exactly as we planned. After gathering the rest of our items, we finish up at the books and toys, just like always.

"Mom, I've been wanting this *Wings of Fire* book. Can I get it today? I can use my own money."

"Yeah, Mom, can I please get this Lego set? I'll use my own money too."

I say sure (mostly because I can't think of a valid reason to say no), and we head to the checkout where both kids put the groceries up on the conveyor belt without being asked. In the parking lot, they help load the groceries into the back of the van. Driving away from the store, both kids give a hearty and unprompted, "Thanks, Mom!" for the items they were allowed to purchase with their own money.

As we get closer to our house, my daughter pipes up,

"It's just awful that he cheated on his wife," circling back around to the plot of *Hamilton*. (My brain is usually caffeinated so I can keep up with her myriad non-sequiturs.) We've talked about this particular topic many times since she started listening to the soundtrack. I reply as I have in the past, believing repetition is the beginning of understanding.

"Yes, it is awful. When you sleep with someone, you share your whole soul. Eliza knew that, Alexander knew it, and so did the other woman. That's why it hurts Eliza's heart so much and why she takes herself out of society for a while."

"Here Mom, look! I pretended to autograph my new *Wings of Fire* book! It looks so real."

Ping! We're onto the next thing.

I glance over from the driver's seat. Sure enough, she's found a black pen and scribbled a fake autograph in her new book.

As we back into the driveway, I hear a groan from my son in the backseat. "Do I *have* to help carry everything inside?"

"Yes, you do," I say as I back into the driveway. Honestly, knowing my older kids will help bring in our Costco haul saves my sanity (and my back) after a long day of homeschool, discipline, prepping food, and shopping runs. They're my teammates—their help is essential for some of the physical labor involved caring for our home and family.

Two minutes later, inside the house, the 3-year-old's tantrum has faded and she's showing me how she can carry all her lovies at once *and* do a jump. It seems like her quiet time with Daddy served its purpose and she's back to a fully functioning toddler. I smile big and say, "Wow!" as I shift from the deeper older-kid car conversations back to life as mom-of-a-toddler. I get a snack for my 2-year-old son, who is just up from his nap and is following me around the kitchen saying, "NACK! NACK!" like some deranged duck. I text with my mom who has taken my 8-year-old son to her place for the afternoon. She texts back: he's finished his reading assignment, and he's loving his one-on-one time with Grandma.

Then it hits me. I am…Pinball Mom.

Switching between littles and bigs can feel like pinball—Up! Down! Side! Other side! *Diapers! Pre-teen angst! Booboos and Bandaids! Laughing together at memes! Cuddles! Watching shows together! Middle-of-the-night bad dreams! Writing assignments! Copywork! Spelling tests! Board books! Chapter books!*

Sometimes my interactions with my children are about stealing mints and hiding in Mama's van and time-outs and opening snacks. Other times, they're about the sacredness of marriage or the definition of a highly nuanced word.

Hear me: I will never tire of the opportunity to help guide and instruct my little kids. But the time I've already spent guiding and instructing the older ones when they were little is starting to pay off in a way I never imagined. The discussions we are able to have now and the jokes we can share together make all of the work I put in years ago seem worth it. This motivates me as I continue to guide and instruct my younger two babes.

My older children serve as a welcome change of pace from the slog of the little years. The big kids also require a lot more deep thinking, consideration, and late-night chat sessions. After years of *only* littles, I am up for the challenge of these new older realms, but still able to ping back to witness the wonder of the preschool years.

I am rocking my 3-year-old little girl before bed—the thief who stole the van mints earlier today. Her brother (the deranged duck) is already asleep across the room. We quietly sing "My God Is So Big," and I brush her hair away from her face and kiss her and tell her how much I love her: "Forever, no matter what." As we rock, her big sister comes into the room.

"Mom," she whispers, "will you come into my room next and scratch my back?"

"Sure, sweetie."

I am, after all, Pinball Mom.

# PART VI

# DEATH BY CARTWHEEL

*Jennifer Van Winkle*

S HE BOUNDS AROUND THE CORNER OF THE KITCHEN island with her usual exuberance.

"Mama, what is a cartwheel?"

My husband and I glance at each other and smile, because this is par for the course for our little wonder-girl. "It's a...hmm," I say as I dry my wet hands on the dishcloth hanging from the oven handle. She looks at me with enthusiastic patience. I am taken with her ability to pause long enough to hear my answer. *She really wants to know.*

I run through the file in my mind of memories that contain cartwheels. I locate a few dusty memories, most of them in the "Vintage" section of my brain—mashed between Care Bears and Whitney Houston cassette tapes.

"Well, sweetie, a cartwheel is a move in gymnastics." She says nothing; her silence urges me to elaborate. "Pretend your body is in a wheel, and when the wheel rolls, the body rolls along with it." *I have no idea how to explain a cartwheel.* She is quiet, not sad, but I can perceive her disappointment in my explanation as she turns to leave. "You know, sweetie, I'll just show you."

My husband's eyebrows shoot up and his smile widens. I whisper to him as I pass by, "I haven't done one of these in a while." My daughter hops up and down amid effervescent giggles. I slide open the screen door to the backyard, and my husband calls out, "Warm up first. I don't want to take you to the hospital." His comment is at the same time playful and full of good sense. *Yeah, a warm-up is a good idea. I wouldn't have thought to do that.*

I find a place in the grass with a lot of room and turn back to address my daughter. "Now you sit there on the deck with Daddy." No instructions in the world have ever been met with such cooperation from both man and child. What a captive audience I have just made.

*A warm-up. Now what would that look like?*

I have no mental images of gymnasts limbering up for a cartwheel. I reason that because I'll be going upside-down, my arms will take the brunt of the force. I twist my torso from side to side and wave my arms a couple of times.

*There. That's probably good.*

I turn to the side with my arms above my head in a Y-shape, then I stop short and tuck in my shirt. I've seen girls do that on the playground when I drop the kids off at school; it seems like a prudent choice. Shirt and cardigan tucked awkwardly into my pants, I resemble an old man who forgot his belt. My arms resume the ready position. "Okay. Watch this."

I cycle my right hand down to the ground, followed by my left, while swinging my left leg up into the sky, and then the right leg.

Before the right leg came off the ground, I imagine

myself looking powerful and graceful. I am mostly done with the cartwheel, just one more leg to swing off the ground—and it stands to reason that the last leg would be the easiest. I mean it *is* last. But cartwheels are not the same as a 100-meter dash, the race I lost many times as a kid. I find out moments later that the last leg to go over in a cartwheel is kind of important.

My right leg surges off the ground and zings in an arc following the other three limbs, and just before it hits the ground the muscle in my right glute and hamstring seize and cramp. *Please don't let me end up in the hospital because of a cartwheel.*

I land the cartwheel on my feet, thankfully. My husband and daughter clap. "Wow, look at Mommy." "Yay! Mommy did a cartwheel!"

"Were my legs straight?" I asked with excitement. I don't want to be one of those women who think they are doing a real cartwheel but they actually look more like an ostrich trying to get its head dislodged from a hole in the ground. All booty and no legs in the air.

"Um...kinda," my husband says. His clapping slows down as he thinks about the ramifications of his answer. *Dang it.* By now the cramp glues my muscle in a death grip around the bone like a student driver white-knuckling a steering wheel. I subtly rub my right butt cheek and casually say, "The legs have more to do with a cartwheel than I remember."

My husband nods his head, even though he's never done a cartwheel in his life. "Yeah, the energy has to come from somewhere...wait, what are you doing?"

Not knowing when to leave well enough alone, I return to my starting place for a second cartwheel.

"I'm going to do another one," I say matter-of-factly, twisting my right toes back and forth into the grass, solidifying my grip and my resolve.

I've never been described as a person lacking energy. I feel the need to prove to him and my daughter that I've got energy in every fiber, even leg-fiber. I desperately want my legs to be straight, drawing a beautiful arc in the air. I figure my legs are warmed up now, so it will probably go better this time.

I spin hand over hand for a second time with plenty of leg gusto, but the cramp radiates up my torso into my right arm. *Oh please don't land on your head!* I crash into a patch of clover, squashing my intentions for a flawless exhibition right under my bum. So much for being the image of gymnastic grace for my daughter. I laugh, pretending I have not hurt myself. "So...that's a cartwheel."

I head back to the house without making eye contact with my husband and daughter. I'm afraid he will see the pain written on my face. I don't want to hear an "I told you so." Behind me I hear my daughter shouting with exuberance, "Yay! That's a cartwheel! Mommy did a cartwheel!" Moments ago, she and I were running on the same bright, joy-filled fuel, but my tank must have been punctured when I landed on the ground. One misjudged stunt left me dry and empty of happiness because I failed—my body failed.

*Just walk it off.*

*It will get better if you just stretch it.*

*You're making this into a bigger thing than it really is.*

*Things will be different in the morning.*

Things *are* different. I wake up, take one step out of bed, and the cramp is still there—maybe a little stronger than the night before. It is a stubborn pain in the...well, you know.

I limp down the hall to the living room. Sitting on the carpet with my legs out in front of me, reaching for my toes, I find it difficult to keep from audibly groaning. My daughter skip-walks into the room.

"Whatcha doin', Mommy?" she asks in her cheerful way. I feel a similar sensation in my brain to the reckoning of a hangover the morning after imbibing too deeply.

*Why did I think I could do a cartwheel without getting hurt?*

*I guess I'm not invincible anymore...but maybe I never was?*

"Oh, just stretching," I offer in a sing-songy way, hoping my daughter will not perceive any of the self-doubt in my voice.

My body is a good soldier most of the time. It (almost) always carries out orders as directed. Rarely do I give the capability of my body a second thought.

*I'm almost 40 years old. People of that age have no business doing cartwheels.*

She plops down beside me as I stretch. I extend my poor right leg straight out in front of me and bend my left knee, placing my foot on my right inner thigh. She assumes the same position.

*My thoughts about my body always seem to revolve around the negative.*

I turn my torso toward my right leg and bend forward, reaching for my toes. She reaches for hers.

*I need it to be exemplary in every way to prove it is worthy.*

My right hamstring and glute cry out in anguish. I take a deep breath, attempting to relax into the pain. My heart drifts closer to my leg, increasing the stretch. The physical pain in my legs starts to penetrate the walls of my heart and mind. My muscles begin to speak to my heart as if they had emotions. They are deeply hurt, belittled, taken for granted by the words I allow my mind to speak over them.

My daughter takes a deep breath, and I suddenly realize she is watching and copying my every move. I'm thankful she hasn't been able to hear my thoughts.

*If I don't spend more time expressing gratitude for my body, she might not be grateful for hers. If I don't start verbally praising my body, then she might grow up thinking it is appropriate to have unkind thoughts about her body.*

Something died in me the day I did the cartwheel for my daughter, but something came alive in its place. I am done holding myself prisoner, forcing myself to conform to a set of ideals that don't celebrate my own God-given value. I am done letting those voices tell me if I just work harder, then I'll be worthy. I am done being my own worst critic. My body is there to help me experience life to the fullest, and the way I treat it is a handbook for my daughter. I want to raise my daughter to grow up loving her body for the things it allows her to do. I want her to remember me, the mom who does cartwheels while laughing, even if her legs aren't super straight and she's pushing 40. I've got one body and one shot at this life, one shot at being a mother to a 4-year-old girl. Life is short—I want to live it well.

I'll just make sure to stretch. A warm-up is a good idea.

# HOPE AFTER MISCARRIAGE

*Robin Chapman*

FIVE YEARS AGO, my husband and I had three children and were ready for a fourth. One Saturday, I did what I always compulsively do when we're not actively preventing a baby: I took a pregnancy test a few days before I expected my period. I'm fertile and neurotic and buy pregnancy tests in bulk because if I happen to be pregnant, I need to know *yesterday*, so I had one (two dozen) on hand. Hours (three minutes) later, I saw a faint second pink line. I climbed back into bed, head spinning with calculations—last period, due date, space between the third and fourth babies. I whispered the news to my husband, who was still barely awake. He smiled sleepily, submitting to my deluge of dates, numbers, and implications, by this time used to the manic whirring my brain does when I find (or suspect) I'm expecting.

A few days later, I decided to test again "to make sure." (I told you—neurotic.) That second line, rather than being bright and bold as I expected, getting darker as hormone levels rose rapidly, was barely discernible. This initiated several days of obsessive tests yielding maddeningly inconsistent results. No matter how many times I peed into a cup, willing the line to get darker or reappear, it (and baby) seemed to be flickering. A week after the first frenzied calculations of the estimated delivery date, I began to miscarry.

I didn't cry. I still had three children under 5 to care for, and my brain seemed to be glitching. Instead, I withdrew. My preschoolers, with their tendency to mirror me in emotion and tone, also became very quiet. I managed to keep the children alive, but nothing else—no laundry, no reading, barely any cooking, no cleaning, no trips. We ran out of food after a while, so my husband began to do the grocery shopping so we could eat. After more than a month of this, a friend checked in. Since she had some distance from the situation, she had insight I (along with my husband and bestie) lacked. She realized I wasn't being lazy—I was depressed. Medication and counseling ensued; I got off the couch and finally started to process what happened. *I am no longer pregnant.*

We decided to grieve our baby as a girl, Hope, based solely on the fact that I "felt" like she was a boy and I had been wrong with each of my three prior pregnancies. The emptiness in my body was visceral. She had only been the size of a lentil, but somehow I physically felt her absence, and it took me by surprise. Suddenly I could hardly breathe. After a six-week delay during which my only emotion was numbness, questions fell on me like rain. *Why? Was something wrong? Was it me? Where is Hope now? How do I frame this for my children? For myself?* Yet the truth was embedded deep in my soul: God is good. I knew this for sure.

The goodness of God had become bedrock within

me—the foundation upon which I slowly reconstructed my definitions of my body and self and motherhood. The seed was planted 15 years before when my husband lost his best friend to cancer. He served and loved his friend whole-heartedly throughout the entire ordeal—through diagnosis, remission, relapse, and decline. He was intensely sad, but his trust in the goodness of a God who had everything well in hand remained strong. By the time I lost Hope, that seed had blossomed into a robust trust in this reality. It is not up for debate in my soul. Rebuilding wasn't easy—it was slow and painful and involved lots of circles and backtracking. If not for a sure sense of the solidity of His character, I may not have been able to rebuild at all.

I wasn't sure what this new loss implied about the world or about me as a mother and human. I had questions about theology around the death of babies. With all these doubts brewing in my own heart, I didn't know how to help my big-feeling 4-year-old grieve her ladybug-sized baby sister.

She peppered me with still more questions. "Where is she? Why did she have to die? If she could be small like she was but still be alive, she'd be the best at hide-and-seek. Why can't she play with us? Did she have a mouth?"

I had no answers for her because I had none for myself.

Three months after this loss (so roughly five or six weeks after I started to come back to life and actually grieve the baby), I peed in another cup, dipped another bulk-ordered pregnancy test in my own urine, and watched first one line and then another turn pink while the three-minute timer counted down.

When I saw that second pink line, I instantly forgot the things I knew about the goodness of God. (I know. A literal miracle was taking place inside my body, and this was the moment my "bedrock" seemed to vanish without a trace.) It's not that I believed God is bad, or even that He isn't good; I just didn't think of His goodness at all.

I was terrified. Angry. *I don't WANT this baby, I WANT Hope!* I fumed internally. I was ashamed. *What does it mean if I don't want this baby growing inside me?* Healthcare professionals kept congratulating me on my new pregnancy, making comments about how "it's all okay now" and "pregnancy is the best medicine for miscarriage." What? Just... *what??*

If anything, this pregnancy added to the trauma.

Throughout the first bit, well past the 20-week mark when I learned my placenta was positioned such that I couldn't feel her movement as early as I had three times before, I just assumed the baby was gone. This chorus was stuck in my head at all times: *a few days from now, I'll start bleeding. Then I'll look back at this moment and know I was right.* I had friends and family members tell me, "Once you make it through the first trimester..." or "Once you feel the baby kick, you won't feel so scared all the time."

I stood in the kitchen, 23 weeks pregnant, realizing the baby (another girl) hadn't moved in a while. An hour? More? My heart and brain immediately dropped into a hole of resignation. *Welp. That's it. She's dead, I guess.* I started making plans for what this meant. *I'll need to deliver—she's like three pounds now—does this mean I have to go to the hospital instead of the birth center? Do I need to induce or will this baby come out on her own? How do I tell my husband? My kids? Our families?*

On and on. I wasn't mad. I wasn't even sad, which, again, added layers to guilt. I just *knew.*

An hour later, she kicked. Hard. It hurt, but I didn't care at all. I was instantly in party mode: *SHE'S ALIVE!*

This thing—the baby girl took a nap in utero, I accepted her death, she woke up—happened countless times throughout the second half of my pregnancy. It happened at least daily. It didn't matter how many times I grieved her only to have her kick again, my body remembered the feeling of carrying a child who would never breathe and the emptiness that followed it. My body and mind recalled the trauma more convincingly and with greater clarity than the reality that this baby was always fine.

It was a *very* long nine months. I don't enjoy pregnancy like a few of my friends do, and I was buried in small children and big feelings and *why did I think it would be a good idea to have another baby?*

Even in the hours after her birth, I wondered if she would make it. We named her Lilly Mae, and she was a real human baby no longer inside of me. This was supposed to be my greatest moment: I was eating mint chip Tillamook ice cream in bed at 2:00 in the morning while nursing a squishy newborn with my husband beside me. But her breath sounded weird and fast, and they were talking about transferring her to the hospital because of fluid in her lungs. All of the pieces of a wonderful moment were present, but along with them was terror. Still. Again. Even though miscarriage and stillbirth were, by definition, not risks anymore.

Finally, *finally*, when we got home several hours later, it felt real. Safe (at least somewhat). But I struggled hard with the reality that if Hope hadn't died, Lilly couldn't exist. The pregnancies were too close. So loving Lilly felt like I was betraying Hope. And missing Hope meant I must not love

Lilly very well. *Right?*


My rainbow baby was 5 weeks old before my husband said something that jostled my brain enough to bring the goodness of God back to the front. "You can love Hope, *miss* her, without wishing with your whole being that things were different."

Suddenly, it all clicked for me. *YES. God is good. I don't understand why things went this way. I can no longer imagine not having Lilly in my arms. And I'd rather have Hope in the arms of Jesus than never have had her with me at all, as painful as her loss is.*


Lilly is 4 now. She's sitting on my coffee table, wearing an oversized purple swimsuit with a tutu. She's talking to her slightly-older brother *very* authoritatively, but about 80 percent of her phrases are complete nonsense. "In the center of the earth, you tie a knot. But you write in this book. Writing the energy. You did it on Saturday!" She is her own special brand of delightfully hilarious.

I still wonder what kind of delightful Hope is in heaven. But she is with God, and He is good.

His goodness does not depend upon whether I see it, understand it, or remember it; it simply *is*.

# GRACE COMES QUIET

*Emily Sue Allen*

THIS EVENING DADDY CRADLED YOU IN THE CROOK of his arm, cuddling you to sleep with your camouflage dinosaur pajamas on—the ones with stegosaurus spikes down the backs of your chubby legs. I flicked off the light and left the room. I managed a few stealthy swipes to erase the tears from my cheeks as I made my way around to your siblings' beds for a hug and a prayer. I squeezed each one a little tighter than usual to help me keep myself together despite the sizable lump in my throat.

We held each other before your afternoon nap today, as mom and baby do. I knew full well it was the last time you would nurse, because I've noticed us both growing more content with how things are changing as you shed your baby-like qualities and welcome shades of little-boy curiosity and independence. We shared this peculiar and wonderful nursing relationship for 16 months.

For 16 months, I drew you close and nourished you at my breast.

For 16 months, you held me still and buoyed my soul with your giant blue eyes. While you nursed, you ran your squishy, dimpled fingers through the curled ends of my long hair. I provided the milk to fill your belly, and you filled my heart with joy.

Tonight, it came to a close.

Mothering you has grown me in profound ways.

You were born at night and at home—six days over-due—in the same precipitous way your siblings before you had come. At first, the evening was quiet. Your brothers and sisters were fed and settled. I was tired, and my belly was stretched to its outer limit. It was difficult to find any com-fortable position for rest.

The first contraction was an eyebrow-raiser. No warning, no warmup. The second followed minutes later with just as much gusto. By the third and fourth, I knew you would arrive before midnight, even though I'd just tucked your siblings into bed for the night. Labor crescendoed over the next two hours as contractions gripped and rattled me with rhythmic cadence.

I didn't think I could do it.

*I can't. I can't. I can't.* The thought accompanied each breath caught in my throat, every contraction crushing my courage, as if through a winepress. All I could do was breathe, surrender, and stay the course. One contraction built on another, each one bringing me closer to seeing your face. I refused the fear swirling through and around me. The music of labor grew loud, tumultuous, and I reached the desperate end of composure. A wretched wail tore out of my soul, and then you were in my arms: a perfect, sweet boy laid on my bare, heaving heart.

I cried tears of relief as I felt your newborn body against

me on the outside for the first time; a moment of sweet hush fell after a consuming storm.

That's how it happens. Grace comes quiet, between the swells. Something shifts, and all the thrumming anticipation of what is coming just ahead suddenly spreads out into an open space—where the holy things, stirred in unseen places, become visible.

You smiled at me while on my breast for the very last time today. My sweet boy; joy of my heart. You waved your chubby hand when I tucked you in next to Daddy so you could fall asleep without me for your first night weaned.

For 16 months, I have known this day would come. I've been told babies don't keep and have come to know growth and change are unavoidable. Still, the anticipation of how things must change tugs at my heartstrings, plucking fears that I might not be able to keep these holy moments safe in my memory, though the love between us is truly sewn into my soul in a way that can never be removed.

Everything will be different from this point forward. I grieve moving on from wonderful things and the changes that happen without my permission. I desperately want to freeze, to capture, to keep what is dear to me about you at this moment. I'm afraid once this beautiful season passes, the beauty will somehow be lost forever, and the memories will inevitably fade. Beauty, however, is something of a seed, and just as you grow, so blooms my view of the beauty in you and the beauty in our connection.

I find grace in these holy moments of motherhood— grace to cherish what was good in the past, grace to expect good things in the future.

Son, you are a delight and a joy. You are the handiwork

of God today, tomorrow, and every day thereafter. While I swipe my tender tears away, I will smile and let my heart stretch taught with the enormous love that swells within me, grateful for our nursing season and grateful for the time ahead, when grace will surely come quietly to me in new ways.

# PAINTING A LEGACY

*Lindsey Cornett*

In my grandmother's condo, just off the living room, was a screened-in patio. A *lanai*, we Floridians call it. And on the lanai, a glass-topped, circular dining table with rattan chairs. That's where we sat, Nanny and I, for painting lessons.

I learned the best way to create the illusion of sparkling water is to sprinkle salt on top of wet blue paint, then brush it away after the paint has dried. I learned that flower stems should never be straight lines, and groups of objects are most pleasing to the eye in odd numbers like three or five.

Nanny was a watercolor artist. She painted lighthouses along the ocean shore, white churches with tall steeples, snow-covered evergreen trees, and girls in fields of sunflowers. She painted Florida and New York and the places she dreamed of going. She painted from memory, from photographs, and from coffee table books. And in the bottom right-hand corner of each painting, she signed her name in faint pencil: Ruth.

On a Monday morning one October, my husband Evan and I went to the OBGYN for an ultrasound, wondering if the little one growing inside me would be our third boy or—what seemed almost impossible—a girl. Weeks before, we had decided that if indeed we were having a girl, we would name her Ruthie, hoping to carry on Nanny's legacy of creativity and love. The night before the ultrasound, my mom texted to say Nanny had gone into the hospital after some abnormal blood work. I laid on the exam table and Evan held my hand as the ultrasound tech proclaimed what I almost couldn't believe: we were going to have a daughter. *Ruthie.*

What I couldn't have predicted as I looked up at the flickering, shadowy image of our little girl on the screen was that Nanny would pass away just four days later.

In college, I served as the president of our campus women's leadership organization, and one of my responsibilities was to help plan the Women's History Month calendar each March. We hosted speakers and musicians, organized panels on vocation and current events, and coordinated with other student organizations to arrange a calendar that represented the women on our campus: diverse, ambitious, smart, and on the hunt for meaning and significance. Each March, we gathered to commemorate the hardships women have overcome, celebrate our achievements, and encourage growth of the rich and loving community women create together.

I loved that work, but it now feels like an entire lifetime away. Instead of running meetings, I lead my toddlers on walks around the neighborhood. Instead of coordinating panels on female entrepreneurs, I schedule well-child visits and playdates. Instead of brainstorming marketing materials, I wrack my brain for a different game to play with matchbox cars. I once walked across a tree-lined campus among 50,000 students. Now I spend most of my days within the walls of our home, two little munchkins by my side and one at school down the street. It's not less-than; just different.

I want to tell Ruthie stories of the women who have come before us: suffragettes and abolitionists, seamstresses and writers, ceiling-breakers and brave marchers. But as Ruthie has grown from infant to toddler to almost-pre-schooler, I find myself thinking about women's history a little differently, and Nanny's story has become the one I am most eager to tell.

All her tips about sparkling water, flower stems, and odd numbers, while useful, are secondary to how she made me feel while we sat out on her lanai with paint brushes in hand: loved, worthy, talented, encouraged. It turns out that being an artist is not about mastering technique, but about crafting a beautiful life and legacy that will endure for future generations. So many women have done that through their activism and their courage, through their campaigns and their voices. Nanny did it with her love, her forgiveness, and her friendship.

In our ten years of marriage, we've had five homes, and Nanny's watercolor paintings are always some of the first things I unpack. Finding a place for them on our walls is always a top priority. I hoist my little girl up onto my hip so she can see the paintings, and I point at the bottom-right corners. "See it there, Ruthie? See the letter R?"

And there, in faint pencil, she sees a tiny piece of our shared history.

# PASSED DOWN

*Jennifer Van Winkle*

I FLIP ON THE BATHROOM LIGHT. Everything looks fine from the doorway, but a closer look tells a different story. A faint brown ring encircles the bathtub, flecks of toothpaste cover the sink faucet, streaks of soap smear the burgundy tile countertop, and there is a funky smell coming from the toilet. I enter with a bucket of cleaning supplies in one hand, a mop in the other, and cloths and sponges stashed in both pockets of my trusty yellow apron.

I'm here to tackle the grime of everyday living.

I twist the dial next to the light switch and the overhead fan whirrs to life above me. Experience tells me to take on the toilet first because the cleanser will need time to do its work.

I spray pine-and-vinegar-scented bubbles into every crevice on the entire toilet, even the knobby plastic bolt covers anchoring the device to the floor. Anxious to get away from the filth, I spin around to the tub. The plastic bath toys have been sitting here for a while—long enough for stagnant water to fester into bits of creepy black goo inside their hollow bodies. I kneel to remove the remaining water from squirting sea creatures before I erase the brown crud from the tub. After I squeeze three crabs and an octopus, a piece of sludge dislodges from a plastic dolphin mouth and splatters across my apron, narrowly missing my white t-shirt. I am simultaneously disgusted and relieved: keeping white laundry white is harder than rocket science. I can never know for sure what will erupt from the creatures frequenting my bathtub. The apron is non-negotiable.

Next I turn to the sink, looking forward to the satisfying work of restoring the gleam to enameled surfaces. As I pass the blue scouring pad around the basin, I can feel the rough, caked-on scum disappear into smooth cleanliness. My euphoria ends as my sponge skids over the ragged edges of a giant, rusting gash in the white enamel. I hate this sink. It always reminds me of the things I can't have. No matter how hard I scrub, it will never be completely smooth and clean. I wish we could replace it, but it's not on the landlord's priority list.

Amid despair over my inability to make the stupid sink shine, I catch a glimpse of my cheerful yellow apron again and remember my grandmother and great-grandmother. This time-softened strawberry-dotted cotton hugged both of their middles before it was passed down to me. A twinge of shame pierces my heart as I consider that my parents, grandparents, and great-grands were homeowners long before they reached my current age. My lack of homeownership must mean I am doing something wrong.

I rummage through the bucket of supplies for a stronger cleaning agent, and the shame I feel gives way to apathy. I realize every place I've lived my entire life has belonged to someone else. Landlords, parents, and my mother's womb have all provided one of my most basic needs, but with it came the requirement to adhere to another person's rules and wishes.

"You can't have pets because they will scratch the floors and stain the carpets."

"You are not allowed to paint or hang anything heavy on the walls."

"You have to clean your room before you can have friends over."

"For heaven's sake, don't kick me there."

Even though it is nice not to be responsible for replacing the furnace when it fails or repairing a window shattered by a burglar's bat, I wonder if caring for a home belonging to someone else is a lost cause.

*This sink doesn't belong to me, so why should I care to make it shine?*

I fiddle with the strawberry-red apron strings coming loose from my waist. A question fills my mind.

*How would it feel to have freedom to make decisions without first gaining the approval of another party?*

I stand up and reach into a pocket for a cloth and I notice the vintage fabric is tearing away at the 50-year-old seam.

*Perfect. Add it to the list of Things-I-Have-to-Take-Care-of-But-Wish-I-Didn't.*

*Hey weirdo! You've been complaining about not having enough responsibility, and now you are frustrated you have to fix something? News flash, sister: responsibility comes whether you want it or not. You have to care about all of your crap, even the rented and inherited kinds.*

I pinch the specks of blue scouring pad sticking to the snaggy edges of the gouge in my old rented sink as I wax philosophic. The soft fabric of the apron soaks up the water pooling on the counter's edge.

*Nothing has ever truly belonged to me, or to any of us for that matter. Yet we are responsible for providing stewardship and care.*

Such is life. Stewardship is a human principle. We are all temporary tenants in this world, inheriting everything good, bad, and ugly left to us, passing it down to those who come after. It matters what we choose to do with the stuff when it is our turn to manage it.

I look up from the rusty, wounded sink and see my apron-clad reflection in the toothpaste-free mirror. I inherited this cheerful yellow apron with red strawberries from my grandmother, who inherited it from my great-grandmother. This garment represents a legacy of hard work endured by those men and women who went before me—people who exist to me as fabrications of second-hand memories. They were people who lived by the notion that even small things were hard to come by. They felt the cost associated with every item they wanted to possess. Parting with money was hard. No doubt, the things they owned came the old-fashioned way—through blood, sweat, tears, and doing things that needed to be done, regardless of desire.

I think of Great-Grandma as she sat down to construct this humble apron and wonder about the circumstances leading to its creation. Perhaps she made it to replace one that was threadbare, patched, and beyond saving? Maybe, like me, she jammed the pockets full of odds and ends accumulated from her rounds through the house? Clothespins, hairpins, tissues, and Legos. No, probably no Legos graced these pockets when she wore them. She, too, might have been frustrated by busted seams. Still, she would have mended what was broken rather than toss it in the garbage and pout about not having the best and most durable item money could buy.

Remembering the past is a buoy in a storm. With renewed perspective, I get back to the task at hand. The way a boot polisher buffs a mirror-like finish into leather, I grab the lime green polishing cloth and shine the chrome faucet to a brilliant gleam. I clean this bathroom, not to impress anyone, but to serve the needs of my family. This is my home, after all, even if someone else's name is on the deed.

I cinch the wise old apron strings a little tighter around my waist. The past illuminates the present. I remember I am part of a legacy of hard work that girds, protects, and prepares me to take on the challenges that await—to say yes to the responsibility of stewardship.

And now for the toilet, then a needle and some sunny yellow thread.

# IT JUST GETS BETTER

*Mary Kate Brown*

C OME ON KIDS, we're going to the beach today!" I announced one morning.

My three girls had grown accustomed to impromptu beach days since our move to western Michigan earlier that spring. Fortunately, living west of Grand Rapids meant a number of gorgeous beaches were well within a 40-minute drive of our rental home.

I kept beach gear packed in our minivan, towels rolled in a mesh beach bag by the door, and swimsuits usually hung out to dry on the back porch. Sunscreen was optional. On this morning we slipped flip-flops on our feet, made a quick stop by the grocery store for some grapes, cheese cubes, granola bars, and extra water, and drove to a new spot: Rosy Mound. When we moved, I turned to social media for recommendations from more seasoned Michiganders. Rosy Mound was highly recommended and seemed right up our alley, with sand dunes, a quiet beach, and stunning views. Windows rolled down and music turned up, we drove through miles of farmland while the girls and I sang along to our upbeat summertime playlist. We pulled up to a small parking lot and visitor center and grabbed our essentials. I couldn't bring a stroller because our one-mile hike to the beach included wooded dune trails and hundreds of stairs. We *all* had to walk. We left towels and toys behind and set out on our hike. I carried the backpack with water and snacks as I watched my three daughters run ahead.

Olivia mastered the stairs in long strides. Her once-skinny baby legs were now strong and able to effortlessly carry her over the terrain of the dunes. Amelia followed suit with a tad more caution than her sister. She paid attention to things like bugs that might be crawling by on the path, making sure not to step on them. Eleora brought up the end of their parade, her hot pink Nike cap and blonde ponytail bouncing in front of me all the way to the water. They were excited and focused on arriving at our new destination.

No one needed diapers. No one needed naptime. No one needed me to tote five million things along with us on every outing. I felt light. Our hike through the shady dune woods felt like a new level of freedom. I was taking my children to the beach, about a mile on foot from the car and toilets, with no stroller, alone.

In years prior, I could never have managed such a day trip. Restaurant outings when I only had one child were stressful enough. I despised eating out after only a few attempts at weaving through a tightly packed dining room with an infant car seat in tow, occupying a restless baby at the table, and barely finishing my own meal. Venturing to a secluded beach alone would have never been on my radar as a "fun" outing in that season of life.

Watching my children grow up is certainly bittersweet.

I recall the hours I spent swaying in the darkness, watching my babies drift off to sleep. I would linger, holding their tiny bodies close to mine, praying I'd be able to remember what it felt like years later. We spent a good number of years home, keeping with the pace of little legs, short attention spans, and nap times.

Sentiments like "enjoy every second" and "it goes by so fast" caused me to grieve a little bit of those fleeting baby years. The notion that I'd look back on these days with nostalgia forged the association of their growing up with loss. However, I am learning it is not about what I fear I may lose as the early years end, but about what I have to gain in the coming ones.

Venturing out on solo beach trips in this season is akin to the countless days we spent at home in seasons past— we've embraced the present. As my children grow, I don't mourn the departure from their baby- and toddlerhood, but welcome the newness of their childhood. Along with beach days, I embrace the skinned knees, loose teeth, two-wheel bike rides, elaborate Lego creations, and the endless adventures their imaginations take them on. I look back on those tender moments of the past and realize they're ones upon which our new adventures are built. No one ever told me it just gets better, but I am learning it does.

We climbed up a final set of stairs over the last sand dune before we reached the lake. A crisp breeze greeted us at the top as we caught a glimpse of endless blue water just beyond the rolling, sun-baked hills of sand. We were almost there. The descent down the other side of the dune was easier, and as we emerged from the cool shade of the trees, we basked in bright sunshine. Sweaty after our hike, we splashed in Lake

Michigan's gentle, lapping waves, losing track of time.

Hours later, we drip-dried on our hike back through the meandering, wooded dune trails to our parking spot. I carried my 3-year-old on my shoulders and smiled at each passerby. Sandy, sweaty, and sunkissed, we settled contentedly into the air-conditioned car to head back home. It wasn't long before all three girls nodded off to sleep. I glanced back at their messy beach hair and pink cheeks and smiled, feeling the familiar sense of nostalgia I've felt before when each of them were just tiny babies. I didn't want to forget this either.

# CLOSING REMARKS

*Jennifer Van Winkle & The Kindred Mom Team*

M Y CHILDREN SPILL OUT THE FRONT DOOR AND down the steps like water released from a dam. I follow them onto the front lawn, smiling as they scuff their feet in the soft green grass. The grass is a little taller than I typically tolerate. Long blades are still pressed down in three rough stripes, trampled hours earlier during a game of Red Light Green Light. Their giggles and swirling motion simultaneously fill the lawn and my heart. I grab my phone and begin a Marco Polo video of the happy scene to share with some faraway friends who've been asking for a tour of our new home.

"Here it is, friends. I want to show you our new place," I say, panning the camera down the long gray facade of the front of our house.

My daughter climbs the maple tree at the south end of the yard. "Mommy, I'm a little kitty, and I'm stuck in the tree. Can you save me?"

"Honey, I'm taking a video; I can play with you when

I'm finished. Can you wave hi to our friends?"

Turning around, I find one of my boys scratching a hole in a bare patch of dirt with a stick. He picks up the loosened dirt in his hands and sprinkles it slowly through his fingers. "Mom, it looks like magic," he says, referring to the wispy brown cloud riding the spring breeze.

I scan the garden for my other son and spot his short brown hair peeking out of his favorite place. He is sitting behind a blueberry bush, resting his back against the planks of the raised garden bed, popping barely-ripe blueberries into his mouth.

My husband joins us from the shed behind the house, carrying shovels both big and small, ready for work. "Are you all going to help me dig up the grass for a new garden bed?" he asks, his work gloves dusty already.

His question jostles me from the contentment of watching the children play and back to reality. *I've got to work on the garden.* I think of the old raised beds we inherited with the house, the ones I have completely neglected this year.

I am not afraid to get my hands dirty among lovely flowers, fruits, and vegetables, but lately I've been so busy tending fledgling souls that I haven't had much time for garden patches.

I realize the camera is still rolling, so I walk through the garden and point out plants I am proud of: fragrant lavender, blueberries covered in baby blue fruit just beginning to ripen, and mountain lupine with its arrows of purple flowers pointing at the sky. I strategically avoid the messier parts of the garden—the weeds. I often feel an urge to cover up the unsightly parts of my life, as if tasks left undone are a negative commentary about my competence as a homeowner, as a homemaker, as a *mom.* I worry about the judgement of others. I imagine people taking one look at the mess of my garden, questioning how on earth I've been wasting my time while the weeds grow out of control. But only showing the garden at its best would not be representative of the hard work required. *Time for honesty.* I point the camera at one of the long raised beds.

"I have to show you my weed bed, just to keep it real," I say with a touch of sarcasm to mask my embarrassment. I pan the camera back and forth capturing a veritable carpet of green and growing things. "This whole thing...is weeds." I am self-conscious so I quickly add, "There's some good stuff in there too." I zoom in on a few hardy plants, strong enough to hold their own against the onslaught. "See, there is some sage...it will be taken over by blackberries, if I don't do something soon. And there is some rosemary back there." I scratch my head, my vulnerability clicking by at 30 frames per second. "Last year, the strawberries produced well, but this year I haven't seen any because of...well, the weeds, right?"

My friend on the video call interrupts with an exclamation, "I love the weed bed!" *Love?* Whoa. I didn't expect that. After a moment of pause, I realize her simple comment cuts through my shame and doubt, and lands squarely in my heart. I look at my wild and wooly garden patch and smile, now seeing it in a completely different way.

The weeds and wildflowers are in full bloom. Butterflies flit from flower to flower. A chickadee peeks its head out from under the thicket of vegetation with sticks in its mouth, surely for a nest. A flood of vigorous buttercups erupts in bright yellow polka dots contrasting with deep green leaves. A sea of orange poppies enchant the south end of the garden, swaying gently with the wind. And last year's onions (left in the ground) valiantly tower above everything, their flowering white orbs humming with happy honey bees.

This weed bed—and my little family—is full of abundant life. The weeds are simply evidence of me choosing to nurture the growth of my precious children instead of laboring over a perfect garden. Even though I have not tended my garden in the traditional sense, I have still been gardening, helping beautiful life grow and flourish.

*I love the weed bed.*

I turn these words over in my mind and consider how a shift in perspective prompts a shift in the way I respond to the mess around me. The motherhood years can be unkempt, unraveled, and unglamorous. But like weeds, mothers learn how to thrive despite constant challenges and we bloom in unexpected ways. Through testing, we become stronger, wiser, and more confident.

There is beauty in the weeds, and the work we do in unseen and uncelebrated places is incredibly valuable.

Even when you're:

- Sweeping endless crumbs and wiping off countertops...
- Spending hours of your week preparing meals and washing dishes...
- Cleaning up offensive bodily fluids at all hours of the day and night...
- Learning to accept how pregnancy and childbirth have forever changed your body...
- Re-evaluating your approach to intimacy now that kids are in the picture...
- Crying tears of joy and tears of frustration in the same hour...

- Deep-breathing through one disaster after another...
- Lamenting the fact you can no longer do a cartwheel without hurting yourself...
- Imperfectly spreading your attention among multiple children...
- Worrying you might not have enough, do enough, be enough...

You, mama, are a vision of the most profound kind of beauty there is—a life poured out for others.

Even when you are in the weeds and have no idea what to do—when everything seems hard, and the beauty of your season seems like it can only be appreciated in hindsight—even then, you are a powerful force of love in your children's lives.

As you come to the end of this collection, this is our prayer and hope for you:

*May you see the grace and goodness of Jesus in both the gritty and glorious moments of parenthood. May you boldly step into the calling to love, nurture, steward, and shepherd your children. And may you humbly and assuredly accept these truths about yourself as a mother:*

You are strong.

You are brave.

You are beautiful.

# ACKNOWLEDGEMENTS

Emily would like to thank:

Almighty God for the gift and joy of this motherhood life.

KM Team husbands, the Kindred Dads—Kolby, Caleb, Evan, Andrew, Dave, Taylor, Mike, Jerry, and Brian for your support, encouragement, patience, and love for your wives, especially (but not only) during these busy months of working on the book.

The combined 33 children who provide our team with endless delight, content for essays, gray hairs, and hard-won wisdom.

The contributors to this volume and current members of the Kindred Mom team—You ladies have labored, loved, painstakingly revised your work, edited this volume over and over, again and again. Thank you for dreaming with me, fielding wild ideas, saying yes, praying with faith, and writing with heart.

- *Jennifer Van Winkle*—Thank you for your tireless work on this volume and for the years Kindred Mom has been online. Thank you also for the priceless friendship you have extended to me for over 20 years.

- *Lynne Patti*—You are precious to me. Your prayers, your enduring friendship, and your ongoing counsel have been a true gift. I'm so proud of what you've shared in this book, and the book trailer: perfection.

- *Lindsey Cornett*—Thanks for your early and ongoing support of Kindred Mom, and for your encourage-ment through my ups and downs these past two years. I am continually grateful for the way you anticipate what I need, and your faithfulness to every small task.

- *Robin Chapman*—I am grateful for your freaking relentless help, emdash and comma skills, and your resilience. Thanks for *everything,* including the times you make me laugh via a spreadsheet.

- *Mary Kate Brown*—Your enthusiasm, meeting organization, and amazing natural product recommendations are the bomb dot com. Thanks also for being our fearless launch team leader!

- *Jacelya Jones*—I am constantly in awe of you, grateful for your help with Kindred Mom audio, and your Marco Polo smile is forever etched in my soul. Thanks for your grace, your courage, and your inspiring desire to learn everything you can about everything you encounter. I love that about you.

- *Melissa Hogarty*—Thank you for caring about the smallest details in this book and hopping on this crazy train with us. You are a gift to me and to our team, and I'm certain this book would not be nearly as lovely without the attention you have given it.

- *Bethany McMillon*—I'm so grateful for your tender stories and the positivity you bring to everything we do. Thank you, thank you, thank you.

Adriel Booker—Our team cannot thank you enough for believing in us and for writing the foreword to this book. Thanks a million times.

To the talented women who endorsed this book—Thank you from the bottom of my heart for your support, encouragement, and the kind words you've shared about our work: Dorina Lazo Gilmore-Young, Shauna Letellier, Meg Tietz, Becky Kiefe, and Bethany Bergman.

K.C. Ireton—For your support and encouragement through every stage of this project. You're one of my heroes and a tremendous writing buddy. Let's keep writing the dreams of our hearts.

Thank you to our Kindred Mom community—Blog contributors, writers-in-residence, subscribers, group members, Instagram followers, podcast listeners, strategic partners, and all the women who have linked arms with us to encourage moms.

Special thanks to family & friends:

My husband—You're the best bearded cheerleader anyone could ask for. Thanks for funding my wild ideas for 15 years and counting. Kids—Thanks for your patience and grace as I worked on this book. Love you all to the moon.

My mom, Robin—For nurturing me in my earliest years. Kathy—for raising a remarkable son. Lori—for your encouragement and love. My Grandmas: Shirley, Peggy, Barbara, Carroll—your love has produced a legacy that will live generations in the future. Thank you.

Dad—Every time you watch the sunset, be reminded of the things you already know. Life and breath and peace. PJ—You're a treasure. Keith—Thanks for loving our kids. Grandpa Roy—Grateful for you. Papa & GMac—You are missed. Caleb, Lucas & Tavia, Kaleb & Danielle, McKenzie—love you all.

Cindie Brown—You've been there for some of my most tender motherhood moments. Thanks for your compassionate care. Cathy Hayashi—For the many gifts delivered to me through our time together, I am forever grateful.

The courageous women who have held me up through each season of motherhood in your own unique ways— Sarah Allard, Marilynn Song Harri, Courtney Frye, Lora Cook, Jan Coleman, Jane McCaslin, Jackie Wilson, Jenny Rose Wilson, Breanna Winslow, Hillary Smiley, Amy Ganz, Kayleigh Rayment, Michelle Layton, Christy Parry, Angie Burke, Kimberlee Ireton, Lexie Stratman, Charla Vaughan, Becca Ifland, Emily Jodrey, Melanie Escalante, Addie Gerlach, Amy Hanson, Frankie Craig, Stephanie Hudson.

Friends from Community Bible Study, SCC, Flourish, and the Vine Church—Thank you.

Friends from Hope*writers, Rise Up Writers, Joyful Life Magazine, A Wife Like Me, Women Encouraged and all the other ways I've connected in the online writing community. I am encouraged and inspired by you— Kristine Western, Rebekah Fox, Emily Green, Sandi Warner, Gretchen Ronnevik, Bethany Barendregt, Glenna Marshall, Noelle Rhodes, Michelle Diercks, Amanda Davison, Sarah Guerrero, Rachel Held Evans, Christin Taylor, Amanda Dzimianski, Tami Leitz, Tammy Mashburn, Jen Howard, Karen Rutledge, Nina Hundley, Becky Beresford, Heather Lobe Johnson, Charity Rios, Stephanie Cochrane, Karen Gauvreau, Kate Laymon, Gloryanna Boge, Tara Dickson, Becky McCoy, Jen Roland and all the others I can't squeeze into this space!

I am profoundly grateful for everyone who has supported Kindred Mom since its inception. Thank you. Let's keep encouraging moms in the weeds.

# CONTRIBUTORS

**EMILY SUE ALLEN** is the founder and visionary behind KindredMom.com, an online community and podcast dedicated to helping women find joy and purpose in motherhood. Emily is passionate about living a deeply nourished life and celebrating the beauty of ordinary moments. She is forever marked by the rescue and redemption Jesus Christ has accomplished in her life. She lives with her husband and seven kids—three girls and four boys—in the Pacific Northwest. • emilysueallen.com

**MARY KATE BROWN** and her husband left their lifelong home in the Chicago suburbs for a rural property in western Michigan. Together they homeschool their three daughters and are turning their new property into a small-scale homestead. Mary Kate is passionate about helping others find healing and wholeness. She leads an online group teaching the basics of an anti-inflammatory diet, and inspires others to incorporate simple, nourishing, real-food recipes in their own homes. • choosinggraceblog.com

**ROBIN CHAPMAN** is a part-time writer, editor, and birth photographer and also a full-time imperfect mama, wife, Jesus-follower, and normalizer of failure. She is trying to learn how to do this motherhood thing in a way that doesn't land the whole family in intensive therapy. She lives in Fairbanks, Alaska with her four delightful (crazy) kids and her ridiculously good-looking husband, Andrew. • robindchapman.com

**LINDSEY CORNETT** is a loud talker and lover of the written word who lives in Indianapolis with her scientist husband and three young kids. In both writing and life, she explores the intersections of faith, family, creativity, and freedom from perfectionism. She's out there providing hope and solidarity to any other women who find themselves afraid to make mistakes. She is a co-founder of The Drafting Desk, an email newsletter of soulful encouragement for recovering perfectionists. • lindseycornett.com

**MELISSA HOGARTY** is a habitually overwhelmed mama who is learning to slow down and sometimes say no. She lives in Northern Virginia with her husband and three kids, who regularly teach her that she has more to learn in the areas of grace, patience, and letting loose. She can often be found cuddled up with a good novel or pulling cookies out of the oven. She writes a personal blog, Savored Grace, where you can find recipes as well as ideas about motherhood and faith. • savoredgrace.com

**JACELYA JONES** lives in the Chicago area and spends her days enjoying the company of her software-engineer husband in his garden and attending to the academic needs of her older children (13, 11, and 9) with a 2-year-old in tow. She is eager to empower other women to overcome adversity and take hold of the truth of Jesus Christ as they make Him the cornerstone of their lives. Jay is an avid student of the Bible and loves learning new things. • jacelyajones.com

**BETHANY MCMILLON** is a coffee, football, and ice cream lover from Frisco, TX. She adores her number-loving accountant husband and her growing-too-fast boy. Bethany works full-time as a teacher and school librarian, which aligns closely with her love of reading and writing. She is passionate about building deeper relationships with both Jesus and those she loves. • bethanymcmillon.com

**LYNNE PATTI** lives just northeast of Los Angeles in a little suburb called Canyon Country. Her five energetic children challenge her sock-matching skills, her culinary prowess (especially when it comes to boxed mac and cheese), and her ability to conjure the best bedtime stories possible. She is beginning to tell people she is a writer and she almost believes it herself. Lynne and her composer-husband of 16 years love date nights when they get to finish a thought and eat the food while it's still hot. • lynnepatti.com

**JENNIFER VAN WINKLE** is a teacher by training and a storyteller by passion. She is a practiced editor and writing coach who is committed to empowering writers to skillfully enflesh the stories they live and the ones they imagine. She lives in Seattle, Washington with her husband, and her three delightful children—twin boys and a daughter. Life around her house is never dull and full of life—just the way she likes it. • jennifervanwinkle.com

**KINDRED MOM** is a multi-faceted
online community dedicated to telling humble and
compelling motherhood stories. We believe motherhood
is a sacred and beautiful journey of discovery.
Through artful storytelling, we help moms find
meaningful connection, guidance, encouragement,
and truth for the kids-at-home parenting years.

Connect with Us:

**Blog** • https://www.kindredmom.com
**Instagram** • https://www.instagram.com/kindred_mom
**Facebook** • https://www.facebook.com/kindredmom
**Substack** • https://kindredmom.substack.com
**Podcast** • Kindred Mom, available on most
major podcast apps

The very best way to stay connected to our community is
to subscribe to our newsletter!

https://www.kindredmom.com/subscribe

CPSIA information can be obtained
at www.ICGtesting.com
Printed in the USA
JSHW021053190920
7925JS00006B/11